www.pamenarpress.com

KNOCK DOWN HOUSE
KNOCK DOWN HOUSE

STEPHEN COLLIS

Published by **Pamenar Press**

All rights reserved
© **Stephen Collis 2025**
First Published **2025**

ISBN: **978-1-915341-23-5**
Stephen Collis
KNOCK DOWN HOUSE

Cover design and book design:
© **Studio "HEH"**-Hamed Jaberha

www.pamenarpress.com
info@pamenarpress.com

© *KNOCK DOWN HOUSE*

All rights reserved. No part of this publication may be reproduced or transmitted in any form or by any means, or stored in any retrieval system of any nature without prior written permission, except for permitted fair dealing under the Copyright, Designs and Patents Act 1988, or in accordance with the terms of a licence issued by the Copyright Licensing Agency in respect of photocopying and/or reprographic reproduction. Application for permission for other use of copyright material including permission to reproduce extracts in other published works shall be made to the publishers. Full acknowledgement of author, publisher and source must be given.

11
14
16
19
22
32
34
38
45
54
56
59
63
67
68
72
79
83
93
98
102
110
122
124
130
132
137
139
141
149
159

174
178

TABLE OF CONTENTS

KNOCK DOWN HOUSE

HARE, PARTIDGES, WILD DUCK

IF IN SMOTHERING DREAMS

ELSEWHERES AND OTHERWISES

TOOTHPICKS AND MOSS

THE ROAD CUT THROUGH THE INTERIOR JUNGLE

THIRTY SIX CRAZY FISTS

WE HAVE LONG FORGOTTEN THE RITUAL BY WHICH THE HOUSE OF OUR LIFE WAS ERECTED

GATHERING EVIDENCE

HALF IN LEAGUE WITH THE DREAM WORLD

A RAY OF LIGHT FALLS THROUGH A CRACK IN THE WALL OF THE ALCHEMISTS CELL

THE TIME FALLING BODIES TAKE TO LIGHT

A SINGLE STARLING IS NO SUCH THING

THE CITY BECAME A BOOK IN MY HANDS

LIKE THE FLIGHT OF A BIRD THAT SEEMS TO BE APPRAOCHING BUT NEVER ARRIVES

A WINDOW, A CLOUD, A TREE

HOW LONG WILL THE FLOWERS CONTINUE TO BLOOM BETWEEN THE TELEGRAPH POLES?

POEM FOR OSMAN

A SLOWLY SHIFTING ADDRESS

IN THE HALF-LIGHT OF EUROPEAN LONGING

TO SET OFF ON THE JOURNEY I NEVER MADE

A SENTIMENTAL EDUCATION

PROPHECY: A DIPTYCH

ARGUMENTATION WITH REGARD TO THE FACTS AND RIGHT

ARCHAIC PLASHING

OPEN THE WINDOW, FROM THESE LAST DAYS ONWARD I CAN FLY

BEFORE THE SPARK REACHES THE DYNAMITE

TREES COME TO THEIR SENSES

ZOO STATION

VERTIGO SEA

PILOT BOAT

Sources

Acknowledgements

*History is a sewing motion
along a thin membrane*
—Liz Howard

*I take refuge in prose
as one might in a boat*
—W. G. Sebald

KNOCK DOWN HOUSE

One of my earliest memories is of a construction site. I was the youngest of seven children, and as the late, last, and unexpected addition, I got to tag along with my mother as she tried to go about the life she had thought was becoming hers once again. Her friend was having a house built, and we would visit the site; it must have been on weekends, because no one was there working on the house, and I could climb around on it while the women caught up. I wonder how safe that was? I remember a large wooden deck or platform and no walls; the site was up high and exposed, with a view that would have looked out over rocky outcroppings of stunted oak, gorse and broom towards the nearby and ever-changing sea, but I dont remember that view—just the open platform, loose two-by-fours, the sound of my feet on the new wood, the paleness of the spruce planks. Some sort of stage. Some sort of plank in heaven or between the earth and the sky. Perhaps on other occasions there was a bit of wall framed in, an open doorframe you could walk through in an otherwise entirely porous structure that would later form insides and outsides, separate private from more public spaces. Im not sure. But the look of that open platform upon which a house would one-day stand, the piles of lumber, the openness around the site, my running on the boards and the sounds I made doing so, my voice too stuttering out in echo of my feet, sounding the world—all this is strangely vivid, if otherwise surrounded by vagueness and mists. I called it the *Knock-Down-House*, when Id ask my mother if we could go there: *can we go to the Knock-Down-House today?* Apparently from my perspective, the structure could just as well have been coming down as going up, some giant hand perhaps having knocked the pieces of our world about. Sometimes I still think, anything half-finished might in fact be on its way to ruin, and every ruin might simply be an incomplete structure, still waiting, maybe after hundreds or even thousands of years, to be completed at last. The spell cast by the incomplete—the pleasures of the in-process—these have been guiding motifs of my life and writing. I wish I could create an archive of the incomplete—a collection of ambiguous ruins that might be going in either direction—towards wholeness, or towards disintegration, the open question, or even perfect possibility, of the tilt of the times. I imagine medieval cathedrals, whose construction spanned generations, must have seemed like this to those who spent their lives in the shadow of their unfinished forms. Life, perhaps, was that state where you spent much of your time wondering if things were going to ruin or just taking a long time to assume satisfactory form (sometimes the distance between the one and the other is nothing at all, turns on an instant of bombs or bear markets). I guess you could call this a poetics. I dont think it qualifies as a philosophy. But there is a perspective on time embedded in this idea: that everything might be winding up toward some building form, increasing in order and complexity—or that might be an illusion, and everything is actually and inevitably winding down, breaking down, becoming disordered, a scattering of unassimilable elements. From any uncertain and elastic middle, we dont really know which way time flows, or whether it flows at all. We just know therës a lay to that land, a strewn temporality, a possibility of order and a possibility of decay, and the between of us assembled there, wandering amidst the bits and pieces of worlds, wondering if those specs are birds or shells falling from planes so high you never see or hear them.

HARE, PARTIDGES, WILD DUCK

My paternal grandfather's First World War flight logbook shows that he was in the air over Arras, flying his Spad at 3000 feet, on April 9 1917, when the English poet Edward Thomas, somewhere in the field beneath him, was killed by a stray shell, as he stood beside his artillery piece, lighting his pipe. The shell missed Thomas, but the percussion of its passing so close stopped his heart; his body fell to the earth, without a mark on it. It is a characteristic of our species, in evolutionary terms, that we are a species in despair," Max Sebald tells Eleanor Wachtel in a CBC Radio interview. Because we have created an environment for us which isnt what it should be. And wĕre out of our depth all the time,"he continues, living on the borderline between the natural world and that other world which is generated by our brain cells. 'Throughout April my grandfather's logbook mentioned the weather more than anything else: Visibility very bad, very mist—Weather bad, fog"—Windy, low clouds." Yet they continued to fly almost every day, the Battle of Arras unfolding beneath them. Thomas, all of whose 140 extant poems were written between the start of the war and his own departure for the front in early 1917, kept his own journal in the field, which betrays an effort to observe the war from the perspective of natural history. When Thomas looks out at the battle-scarred terrain, he mostly takes note of the wildlife that is somehow still there: "hare, partridges and wild duck in field S. E. of guns"—The shelling must have slaughtered many jackdaws but has made home for many more,"in the half destroyed hulks of blasted farmhouses and barns. Chaffinches and partridges, moles working on surface—moorhens in clear chalk stream by incinerator, blackbirds too, but no song except hedge-sparrow"—"Larks singing over No Man's Land"—"Blackbirds singing far off—a spatter of our machine guns—the spit of one enemy bullet—a little rain—no wind—only far-off artillery." Thomas's ornithological observations become part of the structure of military routine: "Up at 4.30. Blackbirds sing at battery at 5:45—shooting at 6.30."Geoff Dyer quotes Harold Macmillan: "the most extraordinary thing about the modern battlefield is the desolation and emptiness of it all."Nothing is to be seen of war or soldiers—only the split and shattered trees. Thomas, too, commenting on No Man's Land, notes the skeletons of whole trees lying there. But there are always birds, even in the midst of the air war, where the engines of war and the energies of creatures in flight blur: "Enemy plane like pale moth among shrapnel bursts"—"Four or five planes hovering and wheeling like kestrels"—"listened to larks and watched aeroplane fights. 2 planes down, one in flames.'Did he look up and see my grandfather's Spad? Thomas, long suffering from depression, perhaps signed up because of a self-destructive urge; he was in his mid-thirties, married with several children; there was no real reason for him to go.

IF IN SMOTHERING DREAMS

I think sometimes I could measure out my life by the wars I've lived alongside—the moments of bombs falling on cities, invasions over borders, landings on island beaches, missiles launched from land and sea that I have watched and read about and worried and feared and protested. How old was I and what was I doing during Vietnam Grenada Cambodia Lebanon the first and second Gulf Wars Somalia Libya Syria Gaza that time and Gaza this time? And it continues to be strange though it shouldnt be but I think it is—that even as I sit here, quiet, dark, placid suburban night outside my window—even in this very moment of silent thought, on the far side of the planet, bombs are raining down, hour after hour, bomb after bomb, the ordinary of ordinance—and no sound reaches me, no disturbance of the night, no startled birds or shaking trees, no vibration humming through the earth and my heart and mind—no crumbling air and shattered stars—just the witnessless shudder of other lives ending and leaving no mark here in this benighted now, this soft landing of nothing and nowhere, this side of the abrupted earth. How is it possible? How is it that grief stricken cries do not carry across the continents? How is it that the dust-covered form of a young girl, blanched head to toe in pulverised concrete, does not walk straight out of the shadows of the room, from somewhere between the dim books on the shelves, and announce what has happened in our inadvertent names?

I keep thinking about this idea of war, "the father of all and king of all," as Heraclitus defines it. That the war humans wage against other human beings is always also a war against Being, against the Material, against embodied and entangled Life writ large. Against the planet and the planetary. Against the shock and awe of the very fact of shared, embodied existence. Heroic struggle and overcoming do not interest me. My grandfather in uniform or scarved and goggled in the air does not really interest me. My grandfather adrift in the great and ongoing war waged against this thin membrane of planetary life, interests me. "Are we in the middle of war," poet Erin Robinsong asks, "A war with the sea, a war with / the air? Forget the Hobbesian fear of a war of all-against-all—what we've seen unfold is a war of us against all, or *some of us against all the rest of us* (demarcated into specious, often racialized category). Achille Mbembe: "In its dark underbelly, modernity has been an interminable war on life."

In Book XXI of *The Iliad* Achilles, his rage unleashed, fights the river Xanthus/Scamander. Taking watery human yet divine form, the swirling river in a fury speaks to him, chiding the Greek warrior for leaving his lovely streams clogged with corpses, the bodies choking him, and so Achilles plunges into the water, sword in hand, swinging and hacking at the waves, the river surging around him, rushing against his shield, and when he falls back and flees across the plain, battered by the divine waters, the river leaves its banks and surges and floods after him. Heraclitus' war was actually a metaphor for a cosmic, conflictual dialectic of opposites, refined by Empedocles as Eros and Eris, Love and Strife, that shapes our world and produces constant change. I am recording here things I know to paper-over those things I do not, and cannot understand.

ELSEWHERES AND OTHERWISES

The German writer Jenny Erpenbeck, who grew up in East Berlin before the wall fell, considers what her world lost when it gained access to the West. Of her childhood in a nominally socialist state, she writes that the *unfinished present and the vision of a bright future, the destroyed past and the construction sites where the new world was being built, still existed side by side, you could see them any time. Resurrected from the ruins, faces toward the future turned*, that was the first line of the East German national anthem, and you couldnt have one without the other, the future without the ruins." This simultaneity of ruin and construction site is Erpenbeck's experience of East Berlin, and she learned to live with unfinished things ... that it's possible to live quite comfortably in the bottom two floors of an apartment building even when the top two floors have been bombed to rubble." She even writes of missing that incomplete and ambiguous state: I' grieve for the disappearance of unfinished or broken things as such, of those things that had visibly refused until now to be incorporated into the whole." From one perspective, Erpenbeck's longing speaks to the very heart of modernity, where all seems a mass of ruins and construction sites, entangled and inseparable, a time-lapse film of buildings everywhere tumbling down and rising from ruins—whether war or the economy," there seems to be little difference in the end. But there is another perspective here—one from which modernity appears as a uniform process (a project of making uniform, of making everything similarly exchangeable, of making the market "total, global), and from which the fall of the Berlin Wall is the end of difference and the dissolution of the last barrier to modernity's totalizing project. Erpenbeck describes playing in streets that dead-ended at the wall, buildings cut in half, the lights, sounds, and voices of another world coming from over those walls. Even the subway stations of old Berlin were still there, boarded up and their entrances, where steps led down to brick walls, gathering drifting leaves and trash, the trains from the West continuing to run without stopping beneath the feet of East Berliners, who could pause as the sound of the train rumbled beneath their feet, shaking their nearly ruined buildings. Erpenbeck writes: "We knew that an entire world that seemed so close could remain inaccessible nonetheless. But at the same time we learned—if you look at it from another perspective—that alongside the world we knew, right next to it in fact, there was a whole other world," and that the things within reach weren't all that there was. That there were other worlds concealed beneath the earth we walked on, and in the sky where clouds floated across both sides of the city, East and West, undisturbed." The point of view here is one many would likely find unaccountable: a longing for exclusion, a grieving over the loss of a world to which one had no access—of being deprived of the *feeling* of deprivation and exclusion. But from Erpenbeck's perspective what was lost when the East fell open to the insatiable West was the very idea that things could be different, that elsewheres and otherwises actually existed, that what was rising from the ruins might be a wholly new world—rather than just the latest and shiniest, more up-to-date version of the world we already had, and which would collapse and rise again with frenetic, if alarming, consumer frequency. The platform the world was in the midst of collapsing upon or rising from formed an empty space ... for questions, not for answers. And what we dont know is infinite."

TOOTHPICKS AND MOSS

Roberto Calasso, in *The Ruin of Kasch,* describes the scattered, discontinuous, and serial volumes of the French writer Sainte-Beuvës various works as "an immense hallucinatory novel in installments, crammed with rumors, allusions, interrupted recollections, gossip, fleeting images, echoes, reappearances." Sainte-Beuve himself does not disagree: Some people take my essays on authors for literary criticism and complain because my subjects absorb me so. They fail to perceive that in those pieces the criticism is a secondary element: for me, each essay is first of all a portrait, a painting, the expression of a feeling. They do not realize that, forced as I am to write for *periodicals*, I have found and as it were invented a way to continue there, in a somewhat disguised form, the novel and the elegy."Is this a picture of a novel in ruins, or a novel waiting forever to lift itself up out of scattered facts and fragments of research? Maybe there is no difference—which seems to be Calassōs conclusion: Sainte-Beuve after many years had constructed, with toothpicks and moss, that grandiose, excessive, maniacal edifice which was much like a novel but which he would never have dared present as such."

I am also working, here, with my toothpicks and moss. When I first thought of writing this book, at the centre would have been an attempt to fail to write a book about the life and work of the German author W. G. Sebald, which, in its very failure, might in the end be a book most like one of Sebald's. I was too good at fulfilling this aspiration to fail, and nothing remains of this project but ruins. Nonetheless, in the process I had taken myself to several of the locations where the German writer's own narratives had unfolded—walking, for instance, along the Suffolk coast, from Lowestoft to Southwold and then on to Dunwich, tracing the path of the narrator of Sebald's *The Rings of Saturn*. The exercise in repetition and mimicry—which had me stay, as Sebald's narrator did, at the Crown Hotel in Southwold, similarly spending a few days in the Sailors' Reading Room compiling the notes generated by my walk— had, I suppose, the intended effect: the uncanny sense of living someone else's fictional life. More interesting was the opportunity to take in an exhibition of Sebald's photographs at the Norwich Castle Museum. Sebald's books are filled with photographs, reproduced in grainy black and white; however, far from illustrating his text, they function as a sort of counter or sub-text—keeping to Borges' rule that a book which does not contain its counter-book is ... incomplete." The exhibit displayed Sebald's colour originals and various books from which he procured photocopied images. Penciled lines marked cropping instructions, and what he chose to leave out was often as instructive as what he kept in the frame. I struggled fruitlessly for some time to take a photograph of Sebald's photograph of a hospital room window, the protective glass covering the large print reflecting the glare of the gallery's lighting and my own shadow and reflection as I held my iPhone over it, maneuvering for the unattainable best angle. In *The Rings of Saturn* the image—the first in the book, in fact—shows only the hospital window, covered by what appears to be a wire mesh, to which the ailing narrator hauls himself to confirm there is still a world outside; Sebald himself had been in that very room for back surgery in 1993—something that somehow cheered me, with my own degenerating back problems. But in the original print displayed in the museum, one can see below the window, below where the image reproduced in the book is cropped, the shadowy form of a stack of some three or four thick books on the window sill, and below these on a desk or side table, a sheaf of pale gray manuscript pages and a similarly pale gray clay or plastic pitcher. It is a suppressed authorial still-life, and a revelation of that stage of a work's production where its building to completion, or potential fall into ruin, is still an open question. Who knows what material lay there, what work to come or never to be published captured at some particular stage of its genesis, a spirit descending between the stack of source books and the growing pile of manuscript pages below? I tilted and snapped and zoomed in on this ghostly scene of inscription again and again, grainy gray and barely recognizable, but the manuscript remained a blurred cipher, defined well enough on three sides, but the closer I zoomed in, the more it seemed to disintegrate into shadow at the shapeless fourth side, the nearby pitcher a vessel from which some healing draught might yet be poured alone remaining in well-defined relief.

It is also, I now think, an image of the writer's workbench. Tools of the trade. If only I was a more disciplined craftsman! My brother, who enjoys a well-thought out pronouncement, refers to our extended family as *people of the hand*: almost all of us are characterized by the work we do with our hands—foresters, metal workers, train engineers, pilot boat skippers. One brother is a carpenter, another a shoemaker, still another a quintessential jack-of-all-trades (cook, hairdresser, mechanic), and the author of this theory, my eldest brother, a guitarist with sprawling, knotted hands. My sisters, as craftspersons, were good at everything, my mother a highly skilled embroiderer, and my father taught industrial education, made most of our household furniture, and designed and built canoes using the latest technologies in plastics (vacuum form moulds, fibre glass, then in due course, Kevlar and carbon fibre—the scent of resin is the smell of my childhood). Virtually no one was a reader, and certainly not a writer. My father subscribed to two magazines: *Popular Science* and *Road & Track*. All the men in my family, for several generations, have been handy,"all tinkered with machines, followed the technological developments and outcomes of car or motorbike racing, worked on their machines and seemed able to fix anything. Their lives were lived in reverent and loving relation to vehicles, tools, and technology; machines, I sometimes think, were perhaps for them more people than people were, and nothing moved them more than the tender thrum of electricity and metal. They were those in the midst or on the edges of resource industries who had their hands on the controls of trains, trucks, cars, boats, barges—and even airplanes. Theirs was the class pride of being the one at the helm, the one who knew how, the one who skillfully controlled, guided and/or maintained the machine—even if they did so at another's bidding, for another's profit, to whatever ends the machines were directed.

Could I, alone, not be a member of this tribe? To my enduring shame, I can fix almost nothing, barely enjoy driving or care to know anything about how a car works, find most machines and technological devices baffling and alienating. Robert Graves, another poet who served in the Great War, laments his own family's lack of "hands." It is most inconvenient to have been born into the age of the internal-combustion engine and the electric dynamo and to have no sympathy with them. My family is characterized by this sympathy, and we seem born at the side of such machines, waiting to grow until we can reach the controls and take up the tools. I humour myself by imagining I am the single member of Graves' clan, isolated amongst my own. I once worked as a deckhand on a fishing boat, largely responsible for keeping a diesel air compressor running on deck. It roared, rattled, and shook with vicious energy, and I was terrified of it. I knew which button to push and which lever to pull, but did so while gritting my teeth and sometimes yelling in rage and terror under the machine's own deafening howl; its brutal noise and physical volatility seemed a personal threat.

But then I take pen and paper in hand, committed for more than thirty years now to an almost daily practice of journaling, working my awkward letters across the page in tidy rows. "A writer's hand is not better than a ploughman's," Arthur Rimbaud opines in *Une saison en enfer*. Poet Tom Crompton, who draws this Rimbaud quote to my attention, also cites Barry MacSweeney's conflation of poetry and labour: "my sole virtue is / in my hand."My handwriting has become illegible over the years, cramped, flatlining into a lack of verticality, a hodge-podge of upper and lower cases that at one time was an imitation of my father's block-printing from his drafting classes—my father, dyslexic, handyman extraordinaire, careful printer because he *had* to be a careful printer, lest everything go to pot. But I cannot imagine *not* writing by hand, and no poem of mine finds its way to the page without first being scratched out, a pen gripped far too tightly in my hand, in the pages of my notebooks. Try as hard as you might, you cannot get rid of the body by way of the mind.

Where did the privileged male relationship to the machine in my family come from? My hypothesis is that it is my grandfather—son of an accountant and shopkeeper who refused the life of pens and ledgers, First World War fighter pilot and POW, skipper, for some forty years, of a coastal pilot boat. He was the original tinkerer with engines, who passed down this love of the machine—a love he acquired while performing the work of Empire, the work of colonization, the work of extractive capitalism.

This grandfather is almost inscrutable to me. And this is the draw. He was a minor player in one of modernity's greatest dramas—the mechanization of war, above which he drifted, his hands on a biplane's newfangled controls. And somehow—against incredible odds and statistical improbability—he survived. His is a point of view largely unwritten. A story in ruins, collapsing into oblivion—or yet awaiting completion. He knew how—and ultimately preferred to be—alone and unremarkable. Maria Stepanova writes: "It is a luxury permitted to very few to vanish entirely, to disappear from the radar." Most of my ancestors have done so; the least successful in vanishing entirely—although he would appear to be the one who put the most effort into it—is my grandfather Collis. Stepanova again: "In our own history the most interesting part is what we don't know." As far as my grandfather is concerned, he is the only ancestor I can know much of anything about—and yet the paltry nature of this knowledge, confined as it is to the records relating to his few years of service ("those little fragments of bone," Stepanova writes, "from which the skeleton of the past can be reconstructed")—is what makes what I *don't know* cast such a long and rich shadow.

I did not know my grandfather. His life and mine overlapped by just four months; I dont even know if he held newborn me in his arms, or cast eyes on my wriggling existence—perhaps at a Christmas gathering, when I was a month old—no one is sure. As the last addition to his list of fourteen grandchildren, he might not have shown much interest, even if we had been in the same room at some point. His life has been as much of an absence in mine as mine no doubt was in his. All that remained of him, as far as I could tell or had the inclination to note, was an old bamboo cane leaning in the corner of my study, and some vague stories told second hand, mostly by my older siblings:

World War I flying ace, shot down and imprisoned, attempted escapes, court martial and death sentence, liberated by the war's end, followed by decades running the pilot boat out of Victoria's Inner Harbour. With no memories of him of my own, everything comes second hand, part fable, filtered and in fragments rescued from the ruins of a lost and forgotten life.

THE ROAD CUT THROUGH THE INTERIOR JUNGLE

On the cover of Susan Howës book *Frame Structures: Early Poems, 1974-1979*, is an image of her husband David von Schlegell's sculpture for India Wharf in Boston: some beams jutting into the sky, the incomplete frame for a leaning wall, a single two-by-four nailed diagonally across the eight risers and the framed but not yet covered flooring stretching out towards some tools and materials in the foreground. I had for long thought the sculpture was "complete" or nearly complete as photographed—its "finished" state being one of permanent incompletion. The framework of a structure never to be. But in fact the finished sculpture—four identical forms, two facing the other two—are covered in stainless steel, their support beams hidden from view. Titled "Untitled Landscape,"they look like four giant laptops, tilted open, ready to be read watched or keyed. The site on Boston's harbourfront was long occupied by the stone warehouses of India Wharf, headquarters of the trade with the Orient"and thus one of the hoppers into which the world was fed and liquidated. The decaying wharf was replaced by I. M. Peïs brutalist Harbour Towers project: two blunt and institutional looking residential towers, for which von Schleggel's sculpture was commissioned in 1971. Modernism as capstone or continuity amidst cyclically flourishing markets (*trade* falling before *real estate* falling before—we are all falling still). The world is vast but confines us nonetheless. Somewhere along our tether we are attached to epic crime scenes, as well as tiny acts of disobedience and short flights of freedom. We need to be able to see both our entanglements and our severings. Close by is a great forest approaching Modernism,' Howe writes. I am trying to see that forest—from a plane disappearing above trees and cloud, or from a boat on the harbour slipping through fog—either way and no matter how fugitive it might seem now that forest will approach again when our wars have finished untitling all of our landscapes.

THIRTY SIX CRAZY FISTS

A letter of recommendation, dated May 11 1915 and written by Francis D. Little to Captain J. Shenton at the Naval Yard, Esquimalt B.C.: 'I' take the liberty to introduce to you Percy Douglas Collis who wants to join some aviation corps.' I walk and think. Dark birds startle from oak trees near the harbour—maybe starlings, maybe red winged blackbirds, on whose migratory paths our lives are lived. Mr. Little continues, noting that the aspiring aviator 'was in Government Service here for some time part of this at Seymour Narrows taking tides.' Eyes on water's surging surface, lifting to the air as though impelled by a gull's angled wing, the shape of its lift in unseen vortices. I dont know where here is. Seymour Narrows would be a wild place then—a thick wall of impenetrable spruce and fir and salal at the tide taker's back, alone on Maude Island, a dog his only companion. The dog's name was Bird. Percy Douglas, or Douglas Percy, at the time of this letter, had just turned twenty-eight years old, somehow still in search of a way out. Or up.

If I Google 'tide taker' I find:

> How do tides work?
> Camouflage pattern tide brand fashion loose street trousers,

The Tide and Its Takers (the fourth studio album by Alaskan metalcore band 36 Crazyfists),
To save the planet, Tide wants you to quit using warm water, and
Why teenagers eat Tide pods.

I assume a tide taker to be someone who takes daily measurements of high and low tides in order to create a record with predictive potential—hindcasting to allow forecasting. In treacherous stretches of water such knowledge would be even more pertinent, and perhaps a remotely stationed tide taker would send in updates via wireless telegraphy but now Ĭm guessing. What is certain is that just beneath the surface of Seymour Narrows—a narrow channel between Vancouver and Quarda Islands and key to navigation in the area—were two jagged rocks, known collectively as Ripple Rock, that at low tide formed eddies in the rushing current—the fastest tidal currents in the world in fact, noted for their turbulent and gaping whirlpools which spun round and round and led into the void. In 1791 Captain George Vancouver called the Narrows "one of the vilest stretches of water in the world"—indeed, Ripple Rock over the years claimed 119 vessels and almost the same number of lives. The turbulent Narrows was tamed," I read, "when the twin underwater peaks were trimmed by explosion," in 1958. "Taming" the earth has been a prominent pastime of our species. Between November 1955 and April

1958, a 150 meter vertical shaft was drilled into Maude Island, 720 meters of horizontal shaft out under Seymour Narrows to the base of Ripple Rock, and then two vertical shafts up into the twin peaks. 1270 metric tons of Nitramex 2H explosive was packed into the shafts; the explosion—perhaps the largest non-nuclear explosion in history—took place at 9:31 AM on 5 April 1958, displacing 635000 metric tons of rock and water, and throwing debris 300 meters into the air.

Footage of the operation, the first coast-to-coast live broadcast in Canadian history—especially the moving of the explosives along the shafts under the seabed—has the look, and soundtrack, of a military operation, as silver canisters are moved along narrow tracks and carefully placed beneath the submarine peaks. Engineers, government officials, and the media then take their place in sandbagged dugouts to watch. Suddenly the sea between two forested islands decides to join the sky—leaping into the air and in all directions at once, in a sort of volcanic fit. Or the sudden descent of thirty-six giants' fists falling at once and breaking the earth open. From another angle rock is heard to fall like hard rain, a continuous heavy pattering as of hail or of gunfire. The forests on both sides of the channel do not appear to be fairing very well. There is no record of the devastation visited upon countless sponges, hydroids, anemones, bamboo coral, flatworms, sea stars, sea cucumbers, sea urchins, limpets, vent snails, mussels, barnacles, gooseneck barnacles, scallops, various crabs, sea spiders, perch, bass, cod and salmon—every creature a key to all the others.

Maude Island, maybe 500 meters across in any direction, is joined to the larger Quadra Island by a mole created as part of the demolition project, long after my grandfather's time there; as much peninsula as island now, it hangs like a pearl off Quadrās ear. Other than the roaring of the rip-tide over the rocks, I think it must have been a quiet place to be alone for a year, in the company of a dog, ravens, eagles, and the occasional bear or cougar. The forest seething all around. What did he think about there? What plans did he make or aspirations form? Quadra Island, early in the new century, could boast two post offices, a school, hotel, lumber camps, mills, and a mission. The We-Wai-Kai band of the Kwagiulth people had (and still have) their village at the south end of Quadra, where they fished salmon year round. I wonder if Douglas Percy had any visitors. I wonder what he thought of taking the tides from their land.

WE HAVE LONG FORGOTTEN THE RITUAL BY WHICH THE HOUSE OF OUR LIFE WAS ERECTED

Maybe this is ground zero for the something I am after here. Amongst my grandfather's documents, spread across my cousin Robert's dining room table, is a weathered leather-bound edition of *Kipling's Ballads*, or more correctly, as the title page within details, *Departmental Ditties, Barrack-Room*

Ballads, and other Verses, Hurst & Company Publishers, New York (1899). Its calf-skin feels almost alive, gives—but resists—at once. On the inside cover my grandfather has written: *D. P. Collis. His book.* And on the flyleaf a page over it is inscribed, in another hand: *To Douglas, love & best wishes, from the family—Nov. 1915.* I felt no small amount of shock and wonder that my grandfather owned, and obviously cared enough to keep for his entire life, a book of poetry—I had never discovered poetry anywhere else in my family before (other than my father's penchant for reciting at high speed the faux-Latin *In fir tar is / in oak none is / in mud eels are / in clay none are*), thinking my own vocation had come somehow out of the void. The November inscription suggests the book would have been mailed then, possibly as a Christmas present—a small gesture of love amidst the strife of war—to my grandfather, who would have only recently arrived in England, his first job driving and maintaining an ambulance, ferrying injured Canadian soldiers from the south coast to Bearwood Park convalescent hospital, near Reading. I doubt he would have had it with him in flight or as a POW, so the book must have remained with his kit, to be collected again at the end of the war, or mailed to the family after his capture. Nevertheless, its preservation, and persistence now, is in many ways unaccountable.

Across from *D. P. Collis. His book,* on another blank sheet, a verse has been inscribed. I cannot tell for certain whether the hand is my grandfather's or not, but I suspect it is.

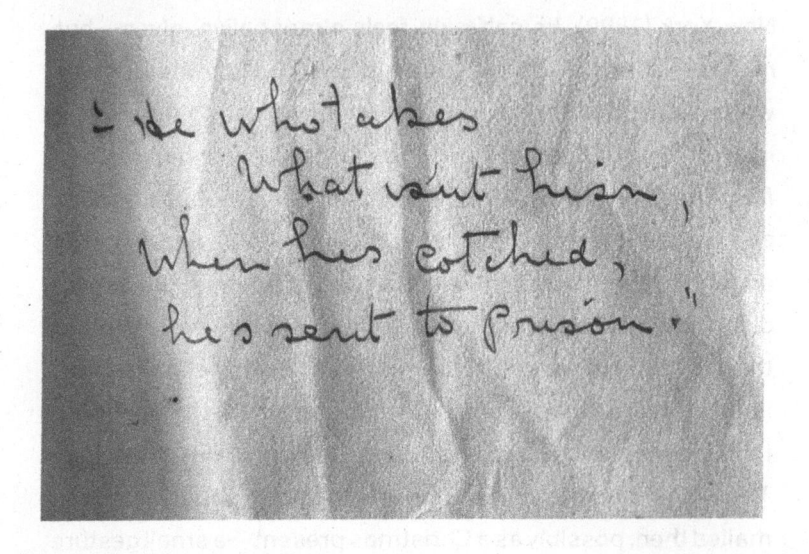

> "He who takes
> What isn't his'n,
> When he's cotched,
> he's sent to prison."

I searched through the Kipling, but could not find these lines inside. At first I thought it might be something added later, after my grandfather himself became a prisoner, but the ink of the pen appeared to be the same as the *His book* inscription across from it. So there is a bit of prophecy there, or a clue to the falsehood of what we dreamily think of as free will. When I Googled these lines my eyes fell immediately upon one particular potential source: a nineteenth century Christy Minstrel play entitled *The Gypsy Maid*. Like other minstrel shows, the Christy Minstrels performed in blackface, and much of the play's dialogue seems written in imitation of the supposed dialect and patois of happy-go-lucky slaves on lively plantations where everyone affectionately calls each other xxxxxx; sometimes characters from works such as *Uncle Tom's Cabin* were appropriated, their original abolitionist message replaced with one that portrayed the institution of slavery as benign. Minstrel shows like this were immensely popular and attracted many of the same music lovers who patronized concerts of Beethoven, Mozart, and Mendelssohn" (according to *The Broadview Anthology of Nineteenth-Century British Performance*); one late incarnation ran at St. James Hall, London, for thirty-five years, until 1904.

Sometimes, things you think you know and have secured away safely fall right out of you, and leave you thin and exposed in the wind, weightless, about to drift away—or, to the contrary, what had been keeping you aloft suddenly evaporates, drops you back towards the earth, spiralling headlong—like Edward Thomas, his heart stopped by something deadly passing within a hair's breadth. Something had been stolen or perhaps forged and passed off as authentic. Something at the heart of what we casually called *culture*. Or society. Was unavoidable— it was after all in our natures to forge pictures of nature, to falsify earthly documents, to pretend our conveniences or trump-up charges. But it was now a time when all our stories were collapsing back into the ground from which we and other temporal beings had arisen—or alternatively or at the same time as confusions reigned, all things solid melted into air—stranger than fiction, strangers to our fictions. The Real nodded, taking the cigarette from our lips, giving us the most perfunctory kiss before laying our bodies out on the ground amidst lavender and bees. My grandfather, inhabited by ghosts, takes up "The White Man's Burden,"a cloak—or hood—of invisibility, recites a racist poem, bows and exits stage left. Kipling, in his propagandistic writings, was an early adopter of the term *Hun* as a German slur, "orientalizing" the enemy as a swarming and savage host: the word appears everywhere in my grandfather's logbook, with its constant shorthand *HA* (Hun aircraft). My grandfather was in many ways ideal British aviator material: born in the UK, toughened up in the *wilderness* of the *colonies*, and returned to the *mother country* for a *proper* public school education. Whatever sort of man he might individually have been, the culture around him was profoundly racist, imperialist, patriarchal, materially acquisitive, and belligerently nationalistic. Whatever real life racializing and repressive terrors those casually quoted lines of *poetry* are connected to, they were, sadly, quite common, popular, and entirely of the class and times my grandfather belonged to. Which of course excuses nothing. Which does not mean such thinking is not still rampant today. What is contradiction but a means of creating contrast, so things may be seen in sharper relief? Why is whiteness so hard to see?

Everywhere we care to look, art crawls up out of the slime of oppression, exploitation, and theft—a patina that cannot be washed off. My brother sums it up grimly: our culture made beautiful things to glorify its own bad behavior. *Our culture, but we cannot stop asking—whose? He who takes what isn't his'n.* Much of the legacy of European art, literature and history falls into this category. Sometimes the statues must be thrown into the harbour; sometimes books will be burnt. We rarely know where to stop, where the line should be drawn—perhaps because that is no longer our decision to make, our line to draw. Rick Bragg, in a *New York Times* review of Emily Bingham's book on the popularity of the song *My Old Kentucky Home:* "the sin was not in loving a song but in failing to understand it." The work is to understand all our complicities, large and small, as between the blooming hawthorn tree overhanging the path ahead of me and the sliver of moon still visible in the morning sky, the difference is only distance. All our illnesses are political illnesses, Peter Weiss wrote, as he began to work on his play *Hölderlin*, after being raked over the coals by the critics for his play about Lenin. There was something inside—something that had been repressed—our family was rife with such repressions—something that made me hate myself—because this is the very mechanism of repression: turning the self against the self—so that in moments of rage and self-loathing I could lash out and slap myself (as Hölderlin does in Weiss's play) as hard as I possibly could—to, I think, harrow or mortify the flesh—as the only way of getting at that which was entangled within it. Etel Adnan:

> **Describe the body**
>   **if you can**
>   **and you will see how unlikely**
>   **your soul is**

GATHERING EVIDENCE

I thought, the world appeared riven with disasters. We are none of us bystanders—to be human is to be connected to a vast web of cascading planetary interventions, expropriations, displacements, oppressions, and extractions—but we dont all stand in the same relationship to any given disaster. I thought, taking what isnt yours might at some level be unavoidable, our form of life depending on our consumption of other forms of life as it does—but taking doesnt necessarily come without consequences, nor does it come without responsibilities—and one can give in return for whats taken. Or ask first. Or have an eye on sensible and sustainable boundaries or limits. If our family copy of Kipling, with its soft, animal feeling and dead body stillness, represented a colonial crime scene, my grandfather was a *person of interest*. But only because the lot of us were also persons of interest.

Kipling is too easy to pigeonhole. The Bard of Empire, sturdying himself under the weight of the White Mans Burden, looking paternalistically upon "sullen peoples," "Half devil and half child," with their weakness for "sloth and heathen folly." If he saw empire-building as a divine mission, he also found the actual British Empire not always up to the task, lacking in administrative resolve, in need of censure and/or encouragement. Millions of oppressed and exploited Indians, abducted and drowned Africans, and displaced and murdered Indigenous peoples might wonder about the *more* Kipling seemed to demand of his Empire. When it came to the Great War, for which he played the role of prime British propagandist, he railed against pacificists and those that would appease the *Hun at the Gate*. The characterization of the Hun—bloodthirsty, bestial, child murderer, epigone of barbarism—was in the end not much different from the way any ejected and demonized Other has been written about from the heart of fragile white supremacy. The only difference, perhaps, in Kipling's eyes, would be that while the Hun might be "half devil," he was by no means "half child," thus in need not of paternalistic British care, but righteous damnation and incendiary destruction.

In a 1905 story Kipling, ever the celebrant of technology and engineering, evokes a future in which air transportation has brought civilization to every corner of the world. "The airplane appears again in a 1915 war-time story, Mary Postgate," in which an RFC pilot (who claimed "it's much safer than in the trenches") has fallen to his death during a training flight. It may be that some 60% of all British aircraft accidents in the war occurred during training, with an RFC estimate from 1917 calculating that of 6000 pilots then in training—one of which might still have been my grandfather—1200 would be killed in accidents before they earned their wings. Kipling's pilot is mourned by the titular Mary, his aunt's lad's maid and surrogate mother, who later in the story encounters something of a double for her lost boy: another pilot fallen from the sky, but this one, she assumes, is a German, still conscious but badly injured, propped up under the oak tree he has crashed down through. She fetches a pistol from the house and returns to stand watch as the "German" pilot (it's unclear whether he is so only in the woman's traumatized mind, or in reality), pleading for assistance in French and broken English, slowly dies. A little blur passed overhead. She raised her thin arms towards it.

When my grandfather was given his Kipling in 1915, what sort of commission did this gift signify? What cruelties was he being invited to engage in, in the name of Empire and Civilization? What burdens was he taking up, what sense of whiteness and its mission did he shoulder and how did calling the German a *Hun* make him not white? Being a White Man," Edward Said writes, "was an idea and a reality." If my grandfather scribbled lines from a popular minstrel play in the book's flyleaf, it's all too clear where he stood. I shudder, not at the shock but at the recognition of where we come from: if Black life, as Christina Sharpe has written, transpires "in the wake," then I come from the people who steered the boats making that wake—figuratively, if not literally, though little that matters rests in that particular distinction.

The Gypsy Maid," where the lines in question are rendered Him as steals what isnt hish / When hës catched he goes to prish,"isnt the only possible source of his quotation. Equally troubling, He who takes what isnt hish, when hës caught, hës sent to prison" occurs in Birds of a Feather," a short story by Alexander Bruce published in *The Clever Magazine* (1903), which contains black characters, Uncle Ben and Aunty Ann, speaking in a racist patois. Other renderings with slight variations—my grandfathers cotched" instead of catched" and on occasion prigs" or steals" replacing takes"—are reproduced (and easily Googleable) in *The Journal of Prison Discipline and Philanthropy* (1858) and *The Poor Law Magazine* (1903), in *The Mill in the Valley; or, The Truth Will Out*, by C.E.M (1885), published by the Society for Promoting Christian Knowledge—a story in which a boy is caught trespassing and stealing fruit—and in a number of grammatical texts where it is cited as an example of possessive pronouns in provincial dialects"(one example being about book ownership) in *The Queens English: A Manual of Idiom and Usage*, by Henry Alford (1888), an example of a vulgar"possessive (hish) in *A Modern English Grammar on Historical Principles*, by Otto Jespersen (1954), and as almost universal in England" in *Folk-Lore, a Quarterly Review of Myth, Tradition, Institution, & Custom, being The Transaction of the Folk-Lore Society*. Vol. XXIV—1913. In a slightly more interesting context, He as steals what isnt hish, / When hës cotched, he goes to prison"is cited as a law of England" in Waters Ancient ... and Modern," from *Country Life* (1899), an article on the "matter of our water suppl☐ in Southern England and common resources vs private property (and so, limits on the concepts of thine and mine in the maintenance of common pool resources). Finally, "He who takes what isnt hish, when hës caught he goes to prison" is used as an example of "a few lines of schoolboy doggerel" to add at the beginning of your book, after your name and the inscription "his book," in The Home Library, by Arthur Penn (1883), from a chapter "On the lending and marking of books."

Any of these sources are possible and I know so little about my grandfather so who knows what sort of reader he may have been or if he even ever cracked his Kipling open to read a few verses in an effort to steel himself for combat or seek the relief of laughing at how others differently educated spoke the *King's English* and so rode up high amongst clouds. But there is guilt by association and I know what he was associated with by school and family ambition and those who climb from one class to another are sometimes the most belligerent in their biases—or to quote Kipling himself commenting on settler colonial "new Britons" (he is discussing Canadians specifically) who possess "a certain crude faith in the Empire, of which they naturally conceived themselves to be the belly button."1 sometimes suck in my gut in public to look a little less middle-aged but generally the performance falls flat. Michael Pickering, in 'John Bull in Blackface,"writes: Blackface entertainments in Britain have . . . to be understood as providing examples of natives 'who as 'half devils' and 'half children' were in need of colonial subjection, but at the same time also offering a taste of what was repressed in the name of civilization and the imperial endeavour, respectability and middle-class cultural norms, and John Bull's nationalist pride of place in the world."In The Gypsy Maid"the plantation is a zone of agrarian elementalism" and folkloric entertainment (so *The Broadview Anthology of Nineteenth-Century British Performance* tells me); all the performers are in blackface despite their supposedly being central European nobility with names like Count Arnheim and Florestein. Christ's British company offered an odd mixture of the peculiarities of the Southern or Plantation Negroes in their Holiday Pastimes"with burlesques of Italian opera and Tyrolean folk songs with the singers in lederhosen, feathered caps, and, yes, blackface—all these cultural appropriations perhaps seeming equally as exotic and unfathomably (and entertainingly) strange. Whereas in America Christ's programs featured ... buffoonish malapropisms, piccaninny grammar, and idiot savant folksiness of the most outrageous racism, these were less prominent in Christ's British troupe."The latter mixed anti-slavery songs with plantation burlesque; the heartache of songs like Good News from Home,"about being separated from family by ocean with no hope of ever going back again, was recognizable to many

Victorians" and allowed listeners to imagine voluntary emigration from Britain "at the same time as it invokes the forced separation of slaves "traversing the Middle Passage.

Between the voluntary and the involuntary stretches a very long field or some would say uncrossable chasm or deep ocean beneath ruptured wakes—but more of this in due course. I'm wondering now about prophecy, fate, and karma. If my grandfather wrote the "He who takes" quotation in 1915 as it seems—perhaps only to half-jokingly claim *his book* as *his* private possession—then what ironies or what justice is being served when not two years later he is himself imprisoned although what's *taken* and what's not *his'n* remains to be guessed. If he wrote these lines after the fact of war then does it signal some reckoning or at least some self-aware sense of transgression and acceptance of the calculus of wartime crime and punishment? In war life is *taken* and long after my grandfather was said to stammer and keep quiet keep to himself and let no one in anywhere near what was *his'n* and hidden. In *voluntary emigration* too something is taken only colonial calculus sees no seizure only a long settling in to what was "empty" but never quite home and how long did such migrants look back or upon themselves as merely British citizens on a long march through strange and conquered lands? The "almost universal law" of private property this quotation enshrines was by and large a British invention exported to the world via the taking of what by their own law was not theirs but that's what states of exception are for: lawless expansions of contradictory laws. The xwi lmexw scholar Dylan Robinson, whose people come from lands along the Stö:lō River, at the edge of the delta of which I have lived for well over twenty years, notes that his peoples word for white people, *xwelitem*, means "starving person"—settlers who arrived possessed by an insatiable hunger for land and resources. In his book *Afropean*, Johny Pitts recounts a conversation he had in a Sudanese restaurant in Berlin with a Ghanaian named Mohammed, who suggests that the stereotypical European view of Africans as "lazy" is due to the abundance Africans have traditionally lived amidst, while the white man needs more and more for his life because he is "scared of the possibility of scarcity. Thus the European system is always hungry to be fed, and the more it feeds, the more it wants because it is always in fear of the future."

Ours was a large family and sometimes straightened but we lived in a land of stollen abundance. The mantra was always *the more the merrier* so people came and went in a large family with blurry borders. A family of nine, we took in exchange students a year at a time—Hiro, from Japan, who threw snowballs inside the house (my father's favourite story: walking past Hirōs room while the student practiced German, muttering "ah so, das ist nicht gut!"), and Richard from Kenya, who would go on to become a doctor back in his country and who could not reconcile North American parenting where the youngest child (I was born the year Richard lived with us) was left to loll and roll on the floor while everyone else raced around too busy to be bothered. So Richard would carry me on his hip whenever he was home, or lay me on his lap or lodge me in the crook of his elbow while he studied. I do not believe in magical transferences but it makes me smile that I was in the arms of an African man for much of my first six months on earth—a time period in which my father's father died and the toing and froing of my family never ceased.

And yet what and yet what? Poet Claudia Rankine comments on white liberal guilt at moments of racialized crisis, noting that there really is no mode of empathy that can replicate the daily strain of knowing that as a black person you can be killed for simply being black."This is so and what is ourh may be a legacy of colonial hate and techno-imperial destruction but if we dont all stand accountable to even the seemingly smallest roles played therein then what can we do about the course of history but pick at the seam and unsettle again and again?

HALF IN LEAGUE WITH THE DREAM WORLD

In a dream my grandfather is in a plane flying over an ochre desert. I am filming him with my phone though it isnt clear exactly where I am or how I am getting such a good picture—closeups of the cockpit, my goggled grandfather craning his neck to look down at the landscape below. The plane is pale yellow and of uncertain era or origin. It banks, diving steeply as it comes back towards me, its engine roaring. It looks like he is making a run to strafe the ground before me where, I see, a cluster of tents is formed around a 1940s-style movie oasis: palm trees in pots, a small blue pool painted on the yellow floor. Actors in brownface scatter as the sound of the planes engine roars and the bullets begin to hit the sand, stitching a seam of tiny explosions towards the tents and fleeing people. Later we sit on a cafi terrace somewhere in a European city, discussing representation and hate. My grandfather, like any good movie soldier—with a faux, perhaps vaguely German accent, idly rolling a cigarette with one hand, his other arm missing in action, its empty sleeve sewn up against the shoulder—claims he was only doing his duty: he had no strong feelings, one way or the other, about those he was sent to destroy. Our waiter, by dress and appearance, is an African man, and he too explains that my grandfather had no choice. Later the waiter is guiding me through a vast art gallery, explaining how each work on display was stollen from a different home in his ancestral village. Stollen, or is a depiction of some aspect of his culture or community, some ceremony or ritual costume—it's the same crime in the end. He can name and identify everything, and he does so in a calm, matter-of-fact manner, explaining the object's use and meaning, its provenance and which explorer or which colonial company took it when and at what cost. Far down the almost endless salon a fire silently rages, smoke billowing, but it is yet far off and we are not alarmed. We stop in front of a painting—a portrait of my grandfather in uniform, his hands atop a cane stretched jauntily out before him—and the waiter's voice betrays the first note of irritation: *this* doesnt belong *here* he spits.

A RAY OF LIGHT FALLS THROUGH A CRACK IN THE WALL OF THE ALCHEMIST'S CELL

My theme has vista, I could say, such as the view from several thousand feet, while the world moves on beneath you, inaudible over the wind and the sound of the machine. It's strange how quickly one becomes perfectly at home in the air," my grandfather writes to his parents in 1916. The body of the Spad VII he flew was not much larger than a canoe, and even more fragile, its wooden frame, over which canvas was stretched, likely Sitka spruce from the west coast of North America. At the outset of the war the average speed of a combat plane was 70-80 mph and the maximum height attainable around 7000 feet. Used for aerial spotting and photography, dropping hand-held bombs, and attacking enemy planes engaged in these same activities, the pilots of these small machines carried no parachutes and wore no harnesses, and fliers were often forced to make a dreadful final choice: jump, or go down with a crippled and possibly burning aircraft; some carried pistols with which to shoot themselves should they become a flamer."Airmen often saw their victims die at close range, in a return to a more medieval form of combat, as planes wheeled in the sky as horses once did in the grass of battlefields. A rain of arrows. A hail of bullets. The fear of the unforeseen, the inescapable, the imminent hand of death—nobody could stand the strain indefinitely, and stories of pilots chain smoking, developing the shakes, and fainting in the air are common. Once you see a machine fall from the sky in flames,"one former pilot reports, "you always have this fearful picture in your mind."Another wrote: I' dont think there was a single moment when I wasnt scared to death,'the strain causing damage to the essential tissue of onës being. 'The life expectancy of a pilot was just three weeks, though many didnt last three days—friends disappeared and new pilots arrived almost daily so there was a completely new squadron every few weeks."Engine, airframe, and propeller failures were common, wings folding in or a plane riddled with bullets, their holes appearing in the fabric of a wing like the first large drops of rain, commencing the long fall to earth in a doomed machine.'The feeling of absolute loneliness in the sky would have been almost unbearable. Or an unexpected pleasure. We fliers live in fearful and splendid isolation," a German pilot reported, We cannot do without this isolation and have no desire to. Isolation changes a man's nature.... We hover between heaven and earth."The pilot had to navigate by eye, reading the visible terrain below or holding up his thumb to block the sun as they flew into the light, and then dove out of clouds briefly—and dangerously—entered. What trait, what inner compulsion, made my grandfather seek out this adventure? The more you are up in the air,"he wrote his youngest sister Beth, the more you like it.'I have no memories of him myself, but my older brother recalls a silent and solitary man, trim and tidy, a hand-rolled cigarette perpetually in the corner of his mouth and arm garters on his shirtsleeves who, when family visited, would stay out of the way, arriving at the dinner table last, and leaving first, without a word.

THE TIME FALLING BODIES TAKE TO LIGHT

My grandfather and I are lying on our backs in a great field of wild grass, looking up at the vast amphitheatre of the sky, from which we could have just fallen. I call him Pop—that's what he was called in our family. I'm asking him about flight, and he quotes from a number of books I have already read. It was such an utterly unique thing, to fly—it captured the imagination of the age—because it was the meeting point of an ancient, chivalrous and heroic form of single combat, straight out of the romances and epics of old, and the last word in technological progress and modern achievement. Thus in flight you escaped time, and became truly free. If you were in a rut, here was the thing: leave the earthbound millions behind, and ascend alone on lucent wings into a world apart. The early fliers and inventors were all enthusiasts of bicycles and automobiles—of technology and speed and life in motion. On French aviator Louis Bleriot's first flight across the English Channel, Robert Wohl writes: "In 1909 what twenty-year old male [Pop was twenty-one when Bleriot flew] living within the confines of the triumphant and technologically dominant West could fail to feel the grandeur of this challenge?"The nature of this *challenge*—to become 'soldiers of science and progress,"and to win the ultimate victory over the hostile forces of nature—began to circulate widely in print media. French flier Eugene Lefebvre (soon killed flying), also in 1909:

We are too thirsty for air, for space, and for speed to delay the realization of a discovery that history has been waiting for such a long time!"The aviator was the messenger of a vaster life and promised the "ascension" of our species, the transcendence of the limitations of daily life—a Luciferian ambition to escape from the last of human limitations "and through the assault on time and space, make death retreat."

Early fliers, I tell Pop, were described as poets of the air,"alone in the contemplative sky, ascending to rarified realms in the aether, with each daring act inscribing an epic poetry of technological deeds."The airplane was an aesthetic event heralding a new age for all arts and sciences (Duchamp: Painting is finished. Who could do better than the propeller?)'. We dreamt flight long before we accomplished it, so it seemed to say something about the culminating powers of the (especially Western) imagination—at the same time as it said just as much about the powers of self-annihilating destruction and conquest, of Icarian over-reach and manic mechanization. Nietzsche: And if man were to learn to fly—woe, to *what heights* would his rapaciousness fly?" Italian Futurists dreamed of fusing metal and living flesh, of a petrol-fuelled poetry of carefully machined and accelerating assault. Pop suddenly chimed in with some remembered verses, from something called *The Dying Airman:*

Take the cylinder out of my kidneys,
The connecting rod out of my brain,
From the small of my back take the camshaft,
And assemble the engine again.

That sounds about right I say, rolling over and looking at the blades of grass before my nose. The names of the places where we learned to fly, Pop continues, they were all poetry too—Upavon, Netheravon, Larkhill. We sang songs, drank and ate extravagant meals in the mess at night, because tomorrow could very well be the end. It almost always was for somebody. I sighed, noting that the first time bombs were dropped from a plane was in colonial Africa—an Italian pilot dropping bombs on Tripoli, a scene described by Futurist Filippo Marinetti as 'The most beautiful aesthetic spectacle of my existence.' Let's cite Wohl again: The conquest of the air followed naturally from the conquest of colonial peoples, the exploration of the earth, and the penetration of the seas by submarines. The urge to dominate, to master, to conquer was the motivation that drove men to fly.... The cult of movement required victims." Look, Pop cried, and I could picture his hand in the air. But when I rolled over he was gone, and the only thing in the sky above was a flock of birds—maybe starlings—making their long migratory journey. Perhaps not all movement required victims.

When it comes down to it, what I'm really interested in is not so much my grandfather himself, as it is what he might have been standing *near*: some howling machinery, a hopper into which bodies, continents, and species were being fed, for the Greater Glory; the split and shattered trees of the battlefield, the screaming of horses. Wilfred Owen carried pictures of the dead and mutilated in his wallet—I dont know why. Many pilots kept trophies to commemorate their victories—even to the point of landing their aircraft, despite the dangers, to visit the scene of an enemy plane they had shot down. The broken and churned earth, the shattered body amidst torn canvas and broken spruce. The Great War was the turning point in the history of the earth,"Wyndham Lewis wrote. The *earth*, not the *world*. I wanted to think about that. Somewhere inside this planet are the continent-sized remains of a protoplanet, Theia, our collision with which created the moon, some 4.5 billion years ago. Theia, "wide-shining," Titan daughter of the earth and sky. I told myself, I can at least stand *near* where my grandfather stood, for the records I have are at least partially locative. There are places I can go. The world is not utterly withered yet. Birds explode into the sky near the sea, turn in miraculous unison, direct me on my path.

A SINGLE STARLING IS NO SUCH THING

Said this out loud
for no one and nothing
for everyone
and everything
starry regions
avian minds hovering
you and I are nothing
swarms of particles
constellations
liquidities
governed by laws
fuzzy states between
here and there
magnetic and
clinging to continua

Said this to no one
said this to a bird
swooping pulse
throb and oscillation
I'll have a starling
be taught to speak
but what if all it says

is untranslatable
gurgling and sputtering chatter?
A single starling is no such thing
as one grain of sand or one drop of rain
what is vision—what is harmony?
A swarm is what we want to be
flocking telepathic collective thought
flash out so many minds moving
border crossing seas and mountains
though the starling has
much higher temporal resolution
has affinity groups in sevens
just these nearest seven in flight
sevens touching other sevens
you do the math
fractal and telepathic
navigating by quick norms
I am looking for love in numbers
if I form a flock I am leaving
get my breath by being in sync
tunes me and sets my rhythm straight
an attraction zone / a repulsion zone
and angular alignment
votes being counted
despite the turn in the weather

What is at the limit of the infinite?

What is moving out this mobile mesh
of black purple indigo and deep green
background radiation scintilla of feathers
from out which cosmic depths
stars shoot as million pinholes streaming
to make one bird plumed for night
rise into collective form
of flocks governed by their flock members
of the measure of sevens
of the nearness of wing-to-wing communication
of parables stars and spies of the midnight heavens

Said this was an accident
said it seemed a single bird
abandoned on a hedge
was nothing but an accident
couldnt identify one without many
There is only one quarrel in the world
Hölderlin wrote:
which is more important,
the whole or the individual part?
And there was no one human way
to choose or maneuver

and sometimes accidentally *en masse*
thousands of starlings just will form
the fleeting and fluid image

of one leviathanic starling-of-starlings
is all we ever needed to know of politics
and the impossible
and what was common or
could be commoned
crowd wheeling through dim streets
shouts smoke and breaking glass
the air and its breathing
the covert   the cell
sevens touching other sevens
the street of streetlights lighting
swells through cosmic voids
brilliant dark out of darkness splintering
earths dead or alive or still just spinning
all that is a bundle of feathers in flight
all that is bundled
into the bundle of bundles
Dear friend Hölderlin continues
I need pure tones ...
the philosophic light around my window ...
I think mere radiance   is what we honed
wing to wing   biome to biome

THE CITY BECAME A BOOK IN MY HANDS

A street stretches before me, long and straight. As I follow its narrow course between ancient buildings, I am joined by others spilling from side streets, all now traveling in the same direction. The street slowly fills until we are a throng proceeding, a column marching forward. Some have begun to shout, and their cries coalesce into chants, slogans and songs. Flags and banners appear, signs held overhead—though I cannot read them at first. Soon though I begin to recognize words—only one solitary word printed on each sign. A group of such signs falling together as we flow along would appear to form loose fleeting phrases and temporary short sentences. We are composing something—all of us together, a notation of our movements as we rive forward, jostle and fall behind or push ahead. It could be a love letter we are writing. Or it could be a declaration of war. No one sees the totality, no one knows exactly what it is that we are trying to say. And yet we proceed with raucous enthusiasm, a column of text moving through a city, a book of some kind we write together but may never finish, which we may leave incomplete and in fragments in a broken drawer, in a cosmic desk—certainly no one of us will ever read it in its entirety. For there are an infinite number of potential sentences we may yet form ourselves into.

LIKE THE FLIGHT OF A BIRD THAT SEEMS TO BE APPRAOCHING BUT NEVER ARRIVES

I had imagined I would descend on the Central Flying School at Upavon in Wiltshire from the downs above, having arrived by train at Pewsey, the backdrop of Salisbury Plain falling away below me. This was somewhat true as far as the village of Upavon was concerned; the Flying School, barely a mile east of the village, was itself on ground that rose high above the valley amidst farms and a golf course, so that I had to toil up a long hill at the end of my da☐s walk, with no company but pewit and stone-curlew and wheatear. The narrow road had no shoulders, so when a car or truck sped past, I had to press myself into the hawthorn hedge, which seemed to thicken and become more wild and impossible as I did so, my arm coming away scratched and bloody. As I tried to focus on the traffic coming toward me, a shadow passed over my head, and I heard a wash of rushing air—the sound a sailboat might make knifing through dark water as a steady wind pressed it on. That sound of water burbling against hull, hum of wind in sail, tugging taught. The friction of the elements. I couldnt help looking up—despite the better wisdom of focusing on the road and the thinnest margin I was clinging to—and watched as a gleaming white glider, elegant and thin against the blue sky, shot the road and disappeared over the higher ground to my right, where the afternoon light streamed. Just for a moment I could imagine it was a biplane, and I was cutting as easily through the liquid of time, which was the whole point of my visit here. As it would turn out, gliders were slowly circling in the air the whole time I was at the Flying School; the land fell away gently in all directions, and in the distance, stretched over the bones of the land, other hills rose about me, great fields rolling out towards the occasional copse or hedgerow or solitary tree. Toward Upavon, to the west, the land fell sharply into the Pewsey valley, the downs rising steep again on the far side. From the grass airfield—which would turn out to be remarkably short—the land dropped in most directions, rising only slowly in the distance, rolling and undulating. Lines of hedges. No flat plain. The airfield rode the broad back of a great whale, with other sister leviathans rising in the distance. Edward Thomas described the undulating south of England as a chain of islands, and so it could conceivably be. It was, nevertheless, easy to imagine a small plane making the short run down the grass airstrip and launching itself above the gradually falling land, turning sharply to rise in a circle, lacking the long thin elegance of contemporary gliders, its blunt form shaking and clattering as it fought to assert itself in the unwilling air.

My grandfather would have arrived here somewhere between his acceptance into the RFC (and his instruction to proceed to Oxford for preliminary instruction in aviation)', which was posted to him on September 21 1916, and the awarding of his wings on January 14 1917 at the Central Flying School, Upavon. A postcard of the dining hall at Christ Church, Oxford—sent to his sister Beth in Victoria—is dated October 9; it notes that his table, along the left-hand wall in the picture, is beneath a large painting of Henry VIII, with portraits of Cardinal Wolsey on the left and Queen Elizabeth on the right. I dont know how long he would have been at Oxford, but the course of training would have included a lengthy list of topics: theory of flight, aircraft materials and construction, the internal combustion engine, instruments and instrumentation, meteorology, map reading, officer conduct and military law, and even lectures on etiquette, proper behaviour for officers, and the importance of morale. His arrival in Upavon would have been in dead of winter—his first training flight there is November 21 1916—and the winter of 1916/17 was severe, with wind storms, cold temperatures, and significant snowfalls from late November—the worst winter, in fact, not only of the Great War, but of the first half of the twentieth century. Slowly the solid world was whittled away. In Germany, where the British blockade was causing food shortages, it was known as the Turnip Winter. The long cold season even had a marked effect on bird-life in Britain, resulting in a noticeable and precipitous decline in resident species, the destruction even resulting in local extermination in some instances (all species of thrush and blackbird in particular virtually disappeared for the coming year). Even frozen-out immigrants who sometimes took refuge from the continent along parts of the south coast of England and Ireland found the normally mild winter earth there ironbound, the half-starved visitors too weak to venture back across the Channel, perishing by the thousands.

A WINDOW, A CLOUD, A TREE

Edward Thomas was born Philip Edward Thomas in 1878; like Douglas Percy, he flipped the order of his given names. A walker, ever setting out with "lungs full of morning air," he made his living writing book reviews and travel books and popular histories. He did not make much money—not compared to the long hours he spent on dry research and endless toil with pen and ink. He was much away from home and his perpetually neglected family, and thought it was better this way—on foot or on his bicycle, covering the miles of his research, in flight from dreams of falling through empty space into nothingness. Nothing was better than escaping the city's foul air, noise, hard hats, black uniforms, multitudes, confusion, incompleteness—to escape ourselves."His mood was often dark, and there were violent outbursts. At least one suicide attempt is documented. "How nice it would be to be dead," he wrote, "If only we could know we were dead."

He claimed to love birds better than books. The road was his true field. Where Douglas Percy was all above and below—air and water—Thomas had to have his feet on the ground, roving, stepping out on a country road day after day. "Much has been written about travel," Thomas wrote at the opening of *The Icknield Way*, "far less of the road." Often in his travel narratives

Thomas encounters ghosts, doubles—imagined other selves, some lean, indefinite man; half his life lay behind him like a corpse,"the other half before him like a ghost."Something was calling from within himself, manifesting as another man encountered in a lane, rapt in his own reverie—Oh for a horse to ride furiously, for a ship to sail, for the wings of an eagle, for the lance of a warrior or a standard streaming to conquest." It is something of a surprise to discover that Thomas's own infatuation with the road was often mediated by a simple machine: he was a cyclist, and rode as often as he walked, when he needed to cover ground quickly to meet deadlines for his travel writings. On one such trip, it is his double—the "other man"—who enters a shop in some small village, coming out with a chaffinch beating against the inside of a paper bag, which he duly opens, the freed bird disappearing into nearby lavender.

I begin to imagine my grandfather as Thomas's "other man." Thomas may have been trying to dredge something up from inside himself which he could then hurl up into rapture. Or he may yet have simply been trying to escape himself, into the fateful field of battle—as Douglas Percy must have been too. But perhaps I have this backwards: Thomas may be my grandfather's "other man," which allows me to claim a poetic progenitor (although I'm not sure why I might need one—we all feel we are strange, and strangers, don't we?). As Thomas's spirit fled skyward from his body, did it not drop some talisman in the cockpit of my grandfather's careening Spad? Some burnt and nearly invisible vestment, more ash than mantle? Some still-smouldering poetic fire from deep in the earth he had loved? Or—and it amounts to much the same thing I suppose—have I merely taken from the fact of their accidental proximity, from my grandfather's circling nearly directly above the place (just south-east of Arras) where Thomas fell, spotless in the ranks of the dead, an unbreakable if aleatoric connection between the two 2nd lieutenants, and thus won for myself an extra ancestor—one who was an as yet largely secret poet?

On one summer afternoon I climbed to the top of the Ashford Hangars to where Edward Thomas had had his study and complained of the mists and winds and yet continued to climb here from the East Hampshire village of Steep below to write his country books and histories and travel guides. The way took me from the Cricketers Inn where I would stay along little lanes and ivy-covered holloways, almost always under huge and ancient elm, beech, and oak trees that closed the sky above and rendered the lane a shadowed tunnel through time. Blackbirds sang where I could not see and wood pigeons cooed from wheat fields glimpsed bright through gaps in the forest. Past a little brook my path—a mere rough bridleway now—climbed steeply up Ashford hill. A pheasant rattled its hollow resonant sound and I watched my feet as I placed them amongst loose flints like bones from the earth struck free by centuries of walkers. At the top I caught my breath along the gentler grade of Cockshott Lane, passed

Thomas's Red House hidden behind its tall hedges, its roof looking like the capsized hull of a ship long wrecked there. Out I went onto Shoulder of Mutton Hill, sloping steeply down now, the beech trees falling aside, opening the grassy hillside where Thomas's memorial stood with a view fit for kestrels and airplane pilots, the slope of the hill dropping off sharply and a broad stretch of Hampshire spread before you.

One can travel to see some famous city or building or object or site where some historical event took place. I came here for this view, and to look where Thomas had looked. I would be in Steep for less than 24 hours. I would walk up onto the hangers, wonder about their name, and look off at the landscape below me—much of it woods, only occasionally broken up by visible fields and houses, Petersfield partially hidden there to my right and the South Downs rising far across the valley beneath me. The walk would take just a few early evening hours, and I would be gone in the morning. But there was this view, just as I suspected, where you could be airborne on earth—this is what calling a *down* a *hanger* gave you. What sense they might be hung from the sky, or if they were hollow and filled with ancient and elemental flying machines waiting to be freed from the earth, I cannot say. But the ground fell away and I felt my slow ascent and watched the land beneath me go about its daily round and I was for a moment free in the air, weightless, and while I could see all below I was sure anyone looking up would only see a silent kestrel or kite turning in its gyre.

As the war is being declared, and Thomas has just finished yet another prose work taken on for the money alone, he writes to his friend Eleanor Farjeon: I' may as well write poetry. Did anyone ever begin at 36 in the shade?"He is in Wiltshire, having set off from Steep by bicycle (heading for Salisbury Plain, he imagines meandering along the Avon to the thatched village of Upavon). From here on his road will wind its way to poetry and war, and nowhere else. Suddenly the whole country is tub thumping, but Thomas had no time for nationalistic sentiments or the demonization of the enemy. The birds, he once said, are his true čo-nationals."Despite this, the war would continue to grow inside him, something ďark and chaotic in the brain,"something he could not resist. He eventually enlisted in July of 1915; Douglas Percy had done so in May of the same year. Their intersecting paths were slow to unfold, as they would spend the next year and more on the periphery of the horror—Douglas driving and maintaining his ambulance in the Canadian Army Medical Corps, Thomas, having joined the Artists Rifles, instructing younger recruits in map making and the use of compass and protractor.

Thomas feigned indifference, but when pressed by a friend as to why he had actually signed up at all, he is said to have bent down and scooped up a handful of earth, and said, literally for this."Literally. I think this is no simple nationalism. This is about the earth itself. The war, I think Thomas saw, was a world war only in the sense that it was a war *against* the world (as Svitlana Matviyenko writes, the wars of the twentieth and twenty-first centuries are 'ecological' wars)". Something was changing in him: by July 1916 Thomas had applied for artillery work at the front. When the campaign had begun along the River Somme in June 1916, the bombardment rattled windows in London, 160 miles away. The planet itself was being shook—as if it were hollow inside and rumbling all through its depths with vast unfreed airplane engines. The artillery worked in close cooperation with air-born spotters and photographers. Douglas Percy must have applied to the RFC by this time as well, as documents dated 14 August note his transfer from the Medical Corps to the Royal Flying Corps. Both men would be appointed 2nd lieutenants. Thomas cleared out his study at the Bee House above Steep, throwing papers and letters on a bonfire. Both men must have known they were steering or being steered directly toward the heart of danger. Matthew Hollis: For so long, he had been plagued by indeterminacy, but the war was an irresistible force that overtook the uncertainty in Thomas." Thomas shipped for France at the very end of January 1917—Douglas Percy's last flight at the Central Flying School at Upavon is two weeks later; on 4 March he is flying in France. At Arras, Thomas's map reading skills were of use in the interpretation of reconnaissance photographs brought back by aeroplane pilots.

For some reason I like to think Douglas Percy's sentiments were more like Rupert Brooke's: Well, if Armageddon's on, I suppose one should be there."Brooke, the handsome and popular English poet, born the same year as my grandfather, and who would die before long aboard a French hospital ship in the Mediterranean, perhaps comes closer to the mark when he notes Half my heart is of England, the rest is looking for some home I haven't yet found."

HOW LONG WILL THE FLOWERS CONTINUE TO BLOOM BETWEEN THE TELEGRAPH POLES?

Werner Herzog, in an interview, expands upon the concept of walking: *I' would be careful to call it walking. There is no real expression in English. I would call it travelling by foot. And travelling on foot is something that we have lost in our civilization. But physically we are made for travelling on foot, to move at a certain pace, and to see things with intimacy.*" One thing I would like to know something more about is the journey on foot my grandfather took across Europe at the end of the war. But nothing is preserved; no stories have been carried forward about this traverse. Documents report his repatriation December 30 1918, commenting *sailed for England,* with his arrival in Hull reported on December 31 1918. There are seven weeks between the end of the war and the date of his arrival at the English Channel. Family lore says they walked; certainly they would have had to do so across a Germany spiralling through the chaos of famine, defeat, revolution, and proto-fascist repression; there are some 200 kilometers between Bad-Colberg, where he was last interned, and the French or Belgian borders to the west; the path they took—I imagine them as a small party of former POWs, choosing to stick together—could have led through Frankfurt, towards Belgium and Luxembourg, or, heading south-west, perhaps through Würzburg and Karlsruhe (where my grandfather had been held earlier in the war) and so across the Rhine into France. They might have had to steal what food they could, sleep in barns broken by neglect and war, or in ditches where the dead might also be found, lay low and, despite hunger and psychological distress, keep moving west. They would have been quite desperate. Perhaps once on allied soil they could have found help: medical attention, clothes, food. Perhaps. Even a train to take them the rest or part of the way, though I'm not sure about that. There may have been some convalescent time in medical tents somewhere. I simply dont know. You could walk all that way in those seven weeks if you had to: poets, madmen, artists and refugees had done it before. On summer holiday in 1790, Wordsworth walked from the Channel to the Alps, over the Simplon Pass, and back, arriving in France on the very first Bastille Day, and returning to his studies at Cambridge a few weeks later. Hölderlin walked to and (after a few months unsuccessful employment) back from Bordeaux France, starting and ending in Nürtingen Germany—a walk totalling some 2000 kilometers—passing through Lyon and over the Auvergne in storm and wildness, in the iron-cold night, a loaded pistol by his rough bed. Herzog, in an elegiac and romantic fit, walked from Munich to Paris, in the dead of winter, 1974, breaking into houses and barns to sleep at night, because he had learned that his mentor Lotte Eisner was deathly ill with cancer, and he thought that drawing out the journey to her bedside would also keep her alive all the longer. More recently, Afro-Indigenous artist

Paulo Nazareth walked—barefoot—from his native Brazil to New York, a journey that took him five months, in an attempt, in Rinaldo Walcott's words, to make "apparent the theft of Indigenous lands alongside the theft of Black flesh from land." Walcott's meditation on Nazareth continues: "The feet, his feet, planted in the soil of the Americas and Africa that Nazareth traverses, return us to a claim that is more profound than where people have come from and what lands they have laid claim to. In Nazareth's walk-as-philosophy, to plant feet in the soil is to reinstate and reassert our species as one organism among others on and in the earth."

I have been lucky enough to have known several people who, after crossing the Sahara Desert and then the Mediterranean from Libya, on over-crowded and barely seaworthy boats, and after passing a number of difficult months in Italy, walked and forged their way on trucks and trains to Calais and the English Channel, and eventually through the Channel Tunnel, seeking refuge from a world for them rendered inhospitable. Often they arrive with nothing but the story of their journey left to them. One such individual is Osman, who has become a dear friend, and who has had an immeasurable impact on my life. Not long ago, as he and I sat in front of an audience at a writer's festival in Caernarfon Wales, he told us that he made his long journey because he "wanted to live as a free person, I wanted to live like a human being."I was supposed to interview him, to help navigate the intricacies of language

(English is his fifth) and audience (he had never really done any public speaking), but he needed no help. I opened my mouth only once; Osman did the rest. If I am prone to worry about being one who takes *what isn't his'n*, Osman, for one, insists I share the burden of his story. *Give it away, give it away, give it away* he says, thrusting his hands from his chest outward again and again, as though trying to empty a well that always refills before his work can be accomplished—a sea that forever replenishes itself—"the sea that eats us," Osman says, translating an Arabic phrase familiar amongst Eritreans. The sea across which and into which his compatriots have been disappearing for decades. Something in my own chest made me want to walk over the earth without rest (as Andrey Platonov once wrote), to encounter grief in every village and weep over the coffins of strangers. That, or to sit with Osman, day after day, listening to his story over and over again.

POEM FOR OSMAN

Were I some
long travelling merchant
of the ancient
world hold full
of the blues
lapis from far
Shortugai for ultramarine
Renaissance robes feathers
of certain tropical
birds who sing
crossing seas the
wine dark Mediterranean
all the tribes
and subtribes of
lavendula skying from
corolla blue to
iris to lilac
and even your
blue shirt and
blue flag Osman
I would bring
to port dreamless
sleep for you

freighted with purple
ancient and solar
the company of
common blue moths
something almost starling
or let's say
brothers as when
we first met
ready for sleep
on parallel mats
and you would
have a word
pluck it between
finger and thumb
like an indigo
bunting by its
wayward wing find
words for your
years of sleepless
nights but here
you said gesturing
with brightest eye
here you said
I can sleep
because here I
am amongst brothers

I want just
three words and
the truth which
I think is
just the feeling
of the planet
moving under foot
just three words
Osman you choose
your story is
your story you
tell it best
while I would
simply ride at
its northwesterly edge
like some moon
round your dreaming
sphere casting what
reflective light I
could from my
silent drift humming
blue to purple
in range lavendula
inhaled relaxes the
limbic system short
woody shrub decussate
or lobed leaves

compact terminal spikes
of flowers on
long peduncles native
across the Mediterranean
and Red Sea
shores was this
hardy and aromatic
plant holding court
along the hills
surrounding Keren when
you were born
Osman is it
home that helps
you sleep when
you place a
sprig of lavender
in your English
hat having sought
refuge round half
the turning earth?

Africa moves two
centimeters closer to
Europe each year
no papers will
be required for
tectonic movement no

immigration policy can
stop a continent
Saharan dust sometimes
falls as red
rain across the
middle sea in

The Conscript the
Eritrean novelist Gebreyesus
Hailu describes a
journey from Massawa
to Libya for
Italian colonial war:
at night on
ship it doesn't
look like you
are sailing it
looks like the
land is moving

away the desert
can be oceanic
Ferdinand Braudel records
Didier Brignon's assessment
of the Sahara
in 1707: *one*
must be guided
by the compass

and the astrolabe
as at sea
looking at the
deserts you crossed
on Google Earth
one can almost
make out the
brushstrokes of cadmium
yellow nickel titanate
hansa the sand
waves and currents
painted on so
thick you thirst
for anything blue

Rest in lavender
fields Osman rest
from your journey
through this humble
plants mobile biome
lavender perhaps coming
to England with
Roman baths lavender
from the Latin
lavare—to wash
in scented baths
Pliny recommends lavender

for bereavement Galen
for snake bites
stomach aches gall
jaundice and dropsy
Hildegard of Bingen:
because of it
malign spirits are
terrified John Gerard:
the blew part
and not the
huske mixed with
cinnamon nutmegs and
cloves doth help
the panting passions
of the heart
and prevaleth against
giddiness or swimming
in the braine

Sleep comes in
many forms take
your friend Mikaeli
brother in arms
whose hair you
cut (poorly) shaving
your own head

as penance who
nights you shared
your bedroll with
when Mikaeli was
too lazy to
carry his own
who preceded you
to the Mediterranean
crossing his overloaded
boat going down
with 350 souls
Mikaeli lost to
wine dark depths
his sister too
dead in Khartoum
and his mother
dead (cancer) in
Holland so even
in death the
family cannot be
together thus your
efforts to gather
your family with
you in Cardiff
your mother needing
your care and
your son Hamudi

who when he
was born Mikaeli
said let's give
thanks—*Hamudi*—and
so that was
his name and
you are all
together now and
I recall Naguib
Mahfouz's words: *home*
is not where
you are born
home is where
all your attempts
to escape cease

Osman there is
lavender now growing
in most countries
though it's heart
will always root
along African shores
and Red Seas
dream thrones in
our hearts unoccupied
kept open for
a blue wind

or sudden rain
some birds more
infinite song careen
off the moon
or hill hung
from the sky
as we stream
off the downs
almost airborne a
cloud in each
hand and portents
of travel carried
through our dreams
rooted but also
pulling up roots
casting off the
statutes the lit
nights and harbours
only plash made
by dipping this
pen in blue
to begin again

A SLOWLY SHIFTING ADDRESS

For a decade my travel has been occasioned by the fact that I will be joining the Refugee Tales, an annual walk in solidarity with refugees, asylum seekers, and those who have experienced immigration detention—a project with the goal of ending the inhuman practice of indefinite immigration detention in the UK. We live together for a week, walking across the countryside by day and sharing our stories at night. Wherever else I may go, in the UK or on the continent, it is only as an add-on to the fact that I will be joining my friends on what has evolved, for better or for worse, into an unending pilgrimage.

Through the Refugee Tales community I have met two types of people (a gross oversimplification), both dependent upon one another: people seeking refuge, and people who already have, whether they recognize it as such or not, a refuge of one sort or another. The former come from all over the world having fled where they were not out of choice but out of necessity, because someone or something severed their ties to their communities. Maybe it was drought. Maybe it was war. Maybe it was war and internecine violence sparked by drought and the many aftermaths and burdens of a colonial and postcolonial history. They have all suffered much and lost much—so much it is difficult to describe. Words fail here. No matter how many words we have, they fail. They have known jails in several countries. They have known bodily and psychic harm, torture and injury, deprivation and the constant presence of a death that waits close by their side, knowing it could be called upon at any moment, half asleep but always paying attention. They have walked run jumped swam and been smuggled across territories large and small, watery and dry. They have sought refuge and meaning and belonging, but found little support along the way. And yet somehow—largely through their own agency alone—they have arrived on the doorstep of this other world, open-hearted, desperate only to rejoin the commons they have been severed from, to belong and to perform meaningful work, to give more than they receive.

The others, those with a refuge they know as home and belonging and community, come to serve. To help the first group in whatever way they can. To be the hands that reach out to help their brothers and sisters onto the shore. But it's here that things become strange, or perhaps surprising. Because the helpers in turn receive so much—it seems unconscionable, unimaginable, to receive anything in return from those who have been forcibly reduced to the wretched of the earth and sea. But we do—we helpers, we inhabitants of refuge. We receive the glow of their resiliency, their deeply irrepressible human spirits, dignity, and fortitude, which is what delivered them to our shores in the first place. They came bearing wealth—no matter what anyone says, no matter how it looks—they came with riches in their hearts. We cant help but receive the spark from their charge—it radiates all around them, so you cannot help but be drawn in, to feel yourself being raised up—you who have no business being raised up by those who have been cast down. But this is how it is. The shock of symbiosis. The shock that we are all indeed connected. That gulfs can sometimes be crossed.

Sometimes I'm privileged to think that solidarity is our default human setting, from which we can only be cut off by instruments and institutions of severance. We do not appear in the world already cut-off from the symbiotic whole of existence. We are hacked asunder and thrown to one side—a condition that is taught or imposed. To find our way back to the symbiotic whole we must feel and express and act on our fundamental solidarity. In welcoming those who have been cut asunder as one of our own again, we gain access ourselves to that W☐ we have also lost. We become whole. We come home to our refuge in one another's company.

In *Lived Refuge* Vinh Nguyen writes that "the work of seeking refuge does not end when the refugee is granted political asylum." Neither does the ontological state or deep lived experience of being a "refugee." Nguyen proposes the term "refugeetud☐ in an attempt to take social experiences of marginalization and oppression and recast them as states of being or agency." Nguyen continues: Redirecting dominant perception of this category away from a temporary legal designation and a condition of social abjection and toward an enduring creative force, refugeetude opens up new ways of conceptualizing refugee subjects and the relationalities that extend beyond the parameters of refugeeness, generating connections to past, present, and future forms of displacement." My own experience with Refugee Tales tells me Nguyen is exactly right; our community's project flows from the enduring creative force of refugeetude, and its energies pulse through relationalities that continue to grow and strengthen and expand. My only regret is that our reach is not longer, that we do not have the resources to extend this to all who are displaced. Sometimes it does feel that we cling to one another in an unending storm.

The Danish poet Inger Christensen notes that the Italian word for paradise—*paradiso*—and the word *diaspora* are anagrams of each other. Paradiso—originally the word means a walled garden or protected enclosure—and diaspora, meaning a scattering or dispersal, are at some level one and the same. Or more accurately, the existence of one is the condition of the other. We may have a sort of paradise—call it an island enclosure, a green and pleasant land—but it is surrounded by great scattering, by waves of displacement. And its boundaries are supremely fluid and permeable—that is simply an ontological fact. Because paradise can become dispersal at any moment. And diaspora leads, if chance, solidarity, and symbiosis do their work, to a sort of paradise once again (an enclosure, a refuge—however temporary it may be). As Christensen writes, our task could simply be to slowly shift the address of paradise."What I have come to understand is that Refugee Tales is the slow shifting of an address. An enlargement. A resistance to the endarkenment of our times. A retuning of the relationship, one story at a time, between paradise and diaspora, diaspora, and paradise.

IN THE HALF-LIGHT OF EUROPEAN LONGING

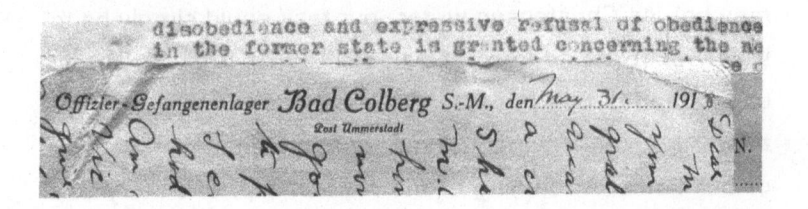

I travelled to Germany one June, to the small Thuringian village of Bad Colberg. I was carried forward by forces I could only partially understand—weak, rather than strong forces, a physicist might have said, but I was attuned to subtle currents of thought and desire. I suppose it was a form of curiosity in the end, although it felt more like the only viable alternative to not knowing and not seeing, and so involved a sort of resignation: I guess I will have to go and find out for myself. If there wasnt to be a vacuum, I would have to fill in a few details—details which would likely tell me little about myself or about my quarry, but the discovery of which I would submit myself to nonetheless. In the end, it was relatively straightforward: after the Refugee Tales walk I flew to Berlin, and then took a train from Berlin to Coburg (where the so-called Coburg Moor—a poorly-imagined and more than a little racist representation of a supposedly African head in profile, like a king on a coin, decorates the town's manhole covers) and walked out of the station and up to the first taxi in the rank.

After a brief negotiation my driver took me to Bad Colberg, a small village some 20 kilometres away, tucked in a corner of rolling farmland, at the base of a forested ridge—were this England I'd have called it a down. My driver threw her car into corners, biting the apex like a grand prix driver, the car's rear wheels sliding sideways at least once; I was relieved when she left me more or less intact at the door of my gasthaus. The innkeeper, who spoke no English, rattled away about what I took to be the usual hotel procedures, including the complex key system (mostly involving how to turn the lock and where to leave the keys once I left, having locked myself out). I got the feeling I was the only guest in residence, perhaps the only one in some time, and the innkeeper had no intention of hanging around. So off she went, and off I went to the nearby Median Clinic—a sanitarium and spa that had served as a prisoner of war camp where my grandfather was held in 1918, and from which he had tried to escape. Today it is a horseshoe shaped complex with a park in its centre, the main buildings looking a little like outsized ski chalets joined by lower barracks-like connecting buildings. Painted pale yellow and with a dirty red-tiled roof, it was surpassingly boring to look at. Its doors were locked, its paint faded and peeling, and no one seemed to be about, although the newer chrome and glass building next door, where a thermal spring fed therapeutic baths, was active enough. I wandered around imagining my grandfather sitting inside this building one hundred years ago, but was not much enlightened. Did he look out here on the enclosed ground, or out the other side, towards the higher, forested ground? I lay on the grass of the park, in the shade of a linden tree, and looked up at the deep blue sky. Birds or planes? Neither appeared. What did it mean that officers were held in a spa? Was prison still prison if the lodgings were not without comfort? I doubted the prisoners were allowed to go lie in the thermal baths. It must have been like being quarantined in a hotel; boredom would be the main punishment.

I left in the morning, hiking up onto the forested ridge along a gravel path, my heavy pack on my back. I followed signs along forking paths to Heldberg, beneath linden and oak trees, brilliant where the sun struck their upper boughs, their leaves still the bright green of early summer. Sometimes I was in the midst of plantation pines in neat rows, wondering about the unknown birds I could hear peeping in the underbrush. It was hot, and because of that, not easy going. But I found wild strawberries, tiny but brilliantly crimson, close to the ground beside my forest path. Whenever the earth offers such free gifts I am overcome with a joy I cannot name or describe. I simply hunched down and ate and listened to the forest and enjoyed the complete solitude. No escaping soldiers ran through my mind. No planes dropped down out of the sky, trailing smoke and history. Clover exploded in dark pink flower and small brown and orange moths lit for brief moments on tree boughs and wild grasses. I was as content as I had ever felt. After some seven miles of this the spires of the Veste Heldberg came into view through the trees, the path now rising up sharply towards it. Built atop a long extinct volcanic cone, the medieval Veste was an almost-fairytale castle of red-roofed round towers overlooking stunning views. My path spiraled the steep slopes, leading up under the fortress walls to a gate beside its tallest tower. Beneath that tower, beside the gate and with a rose bush climbing the wall on its other side, was a low, wide open door and arched entry, through which stairs descended into darkness. Beneath the tower, into the coolness of which I then stepped, was a rough-hewn stone chambre, circular and with a domed ceiling and a bare, cold stone floor. A small square hole was cut in the middle of its ceiling, suggesting another chambre above. There was nothing else there. In the whole fortress I found nothing else that might serve as a dungeon, and so I imagined my grandfather here, sitting in the iron cold alone, storm and wilderness in his mind, losing the ability to speak.

TO SET OFF ON THE JOURNEY I NEVER MADE

Most people, family historian Alison Light suggests, want to know where they 'come from,' an origin. They want that plot of land which will give *them* a plot."One might also feel a little apprehensive about that plot—wariness of plot in fact might be one reason I'm a poet. Family history had never really interested me. I was curious, but only a little, and not enough to do anything much about it: the present and the future seemed anxiety-inducing enough. The fact of my patrilineal lines long stride, so that my grandfather was a true-born Victorian and already a grown man at the start of the Great War, was an oddity, but that's all. Old curiosity shop of time and tides. I knew the *plot* lay in Luton, but also that the Colliss, like so many of their nineteenth century compatriots, didnt tarry there long. On yearly visits to England, Luton would come to mind only briefly—I feared thered be no there there—so I kept away. Until at last I didnt keep away, but decided to see it for myself, the train ride there being barely a half-hour out of London, and the name of the street in which my grandfather was born long known to me. It wasnt even far from Luton station. Cheapside, as the road is known, is only half there now—its sign faded or largely white-washed over, its western end razed, houses knocked down and replaced by car parks, and its remaining buildings mostly abandoned and in various states of decay. Lintels around bay windows and gables are cracked and crumbling, and butterfly bushes— some of them quite large—sprout from second floor ledge work. Some windows and doors are simply boarded up, the signs of long-closed businesses obscured, unreadable. The former Cowper Arms, a "temperance tavern" built in 1882, somehow looks to still be occupied at 53 Cheapside, and next door number 55, whitewashed with two windows dressed in black trims on each of the second and third floors, may be my grandfather's birthplace, if I have read the ambiguities of his birth certificate correctly. A vegan cafe occupies its ground floor (it appears to still be in business, if closed this particular day), next door to the long closed "vinyl revelations"(posters on its windows for gigs by The Cockney Rejects, The Last Resort, and The Crack). The Lea River crosses beneath Cheapside, probably close to number 55; I find it exposed at either end of the old Town Centre, a barely moving trickle choked with weed and refuse, although a few poppies are blooming on one of its concrete slab banks. The present-day population of Luton, inheritors of this urban decay, appeared to be largely immigrant and Muslim.

The next day I followed the Lea further still, up through its Leagrave headwaters, just west of which, towards Dunstable, the true source of the Lea is found in Houghton Brook. Here a distant ancestor—one Samuel Collis, born in Braintree Essex in 1790, and a resident of Dunstable since the 1820s—owned a meadow. I have no idea how large it was, or what he had to do with such a thing as a meadow, but today it is occupied by a shopping centre and huge, featureless warehouses. Samuel's home was at 16 High Street, according to the 1851 census; today the narrow three-story building with its steep-pitched roof is home to a phone repair shop. The rank of narrow and ancient buildings it stands in forms part of Middle Row, pierced by slim bricked tunnels to the lane behind, which has housed shops since the 1200s. I gazed up at the small, arched third floor window of Samuel's reputed home and wondered, where does any of this swimming up streams get me? It's a privilege to be able to, but does it matter at all to see and know any of this? Just a few doors from my ancestor's home is the crossing point of two ancient tracks: Watling Street and the Icknield Way (today High Street and Church), their immemorial meeting point attested to by Edward Thomas in his book on the latter track, which he followed in 1911 in the midst of a deep depression, and which I took up now too, pursuing it onto the Dunstable Downs, where my chalk path immediately crossed five Neolithic burial mounds that held the bones of 4000 year dead people to whom I am likely not related. Was I any closer now, amidst poverty grass and wildflowers, to the myth of roots, the plot that told time backwards as it dug deeper and deeper into the problematical soil? I doubted so. From the steep edge of the downs—where a view of the greenest of green and pleasant England spread open before me—I watched first sleek white gliders from the London Gliding Club, then a red kite, then a speeding sparrow hawk make light of the winds as they cut their paths above magpies and skylarks. They were as mobile as my long lost ancestors, though much faster. There's only so far back one can imagine travelling; further down the line, we become, genetically, both increasingly multiple (how many great great great great great etc. grandparents do you actually have?), and more connected (all of us vaguely related if you look far enough back in time—even to the birds, if we care to go there). I dont think I really want to locate a source; I want to understand the complex of conditions that led my grandfather to war, to Kipling, and to the enjoyment of minstrel plays. Thus I was led back down into Dunstable High Street, to an inn founded in 1540, where one of Samuel's sons, my great great grand uncle Samuel Sherlock Collis, was proprietor of the Saracen's Head. It was closed now—a casualty of the pandemic—but its bone-white exterior had much to say, as did the keystone figure of a turbaned and lushly bearded head above the dooryard. "Saracen" was an early, largely derogatory term for a Muslim. What do the current locals make of this? Edward Thomas also mentions an inn called the Sultan, "which word he defined as 'a dusky king,'" and which he locates in a row of "swarthy, mulatto cottages." Did the "head" in the inn's name indicate a decapitated trophy? Is it just as horrible if it only indicates the appropriation of identity—the use of someone's ethnicity or religion as a caricatured logo? To what crime or casual indecency can I hold Samuel Sherlock Collis? To crass opportunism, and centuries of ignorance and unthought hate.

On my last day in Luton I climbed up onto the Icknield Way

once more, setting off across fields and along tree-shaded bridleways where birds I could not identify sang from amongst the oak and ash. Up Warden Hill I went, with views back down on Luton to the south west, up onto hawthorn covered downs—a red kite circling overhead and soft brown moths flitting all around. Between Warden and Galley hills a vast barley field stretched out, poppies on its edges and skylarks reeling above. A barley field always looks to me as if painted by Impressionists: it's all brushstrokes, all artistry and recreated light. On Galley Hill, where medieval executions took place, I could not pick the Bronze Age barrows out from amongst the hawthorns and underbrush. Just past Galley, as I was about to step onto the Icknield Way—a mirror image of yesterday's walk on the downs on the other side of Luton and Dunstable, heading east where yesterday I had wandered west—I caught up to another walker whom I had seen ahead of me, his head popping in and out of the brush. He stopped, holding something in his hands, and I watched, a short distance off. It was a hand launch glider, made no doubt of balsa wood, plasticine on its nose for weight. The man held the plane high, his arm cocked back, index finger behind one wing and his thumb and middle finger pinching the narrow fuselage, and hurled the glider steeply into the sky. Improbably, it began to circle in a wide wobbling arc and climb. Suddenly I recalled building gliders like this with my father, himself the son of a pilot, and I could feel the light-as-air plane in my hand and I may have shouted something out as my heart shot into the breast of a bird. The other man said something too, but his head was turned away and the wind blew his words away too, and there was little reason to suppose he was addressing me, or for him to suppose that I heard him. On I went along the ancient track, walking Thomas's route in reverse, leaving the other man behind to watch his plane, which looked not to have any intention of ever returning to earth. On I went, up to Telegraph Hill—strange, I thought, that Thomas would die near another Telegraph Hill, near Arras in France, six years after he walked and wrote about the Icknield Way. The track was still just as he had described it over one hundred years ago—and I wanted to feel the shared footsteps of thousands of years of travelers—there is no need for them to be my own ancestors—just common humanity plying our shared way across, and into, the earth. Looking down from the Pegsdon Hills—another lofty drop off downs—I wondered if any of my actual ancestors had been hill walkers with a philosophical bent seeking heights and prospects. I doubted it. They were rural people newly moved to town and upwardly mobile in the first half on the nineteenth century. The census shows that in 1851 Samuel Collis had a servant living with his family; his son Thomas Hamilton, my great great grandfather, had two in 1871—the Wilson sisters, Emma and Elisabeth, aged 25 and 15, respectively. But by 1901 Thomas Hamilton was himself in service, at the age of 68, trying to stay afloat I imagine. For all their efforts and aspirations these men left no legacy—no land, no plot, no ancient pile, no trade or talisman. Henry, my great grandfather, who took his family from Luton to the small mining town of Cumberland on the west coast of Canada, was another climber on the make, and he seems to have fallen just as hard. This is the legacy Percy Douglas turned his back on, stalked off into the bush, into the air, onto the waters—always alone, looking for a way out, seeking silence, seeking a state I can only imagine as a sort of weightless stasis—a ship to sail, the wings of an eagle. These thoughts, and many others, carried me back down into Luton where, as I came along the narrow and tightly-hedged lane of Butterfield Green Road, I passed a curious white house with a round tower and red-tiled roof. Model sailing boats filled its windows, a scale model of what appeared to be a Wright Flyer jutted from the second floor eaves, soaring over the peak of a lower roof, and atop its tower the weather vane was capped by a small penny farthing bicycle.

A SENTIMENTAL EDUCATION

Sebald died having only just begun work—in the form of travel, reading and research, and note taking—the gathering of evidence that always preceded his writing efforts—on a last unwritten project that was to have involved his grandfather's and father's participation in the First and Second World Wars, including the latter's time in a POW camp. He had visited battle sites from the Great War in northern France and Alsace in preparation, and done some archival research in Munich, looking into one Rudolf Egelhofer, a possible relative on his mother's side who had been a commander in the Red Army at the time of the Munich Soviet and who had been murdered by the right-wing Freikorps in 1919. I tried not to allow myself to think I was continuing the German's incomplete project. I tried to picture my grandfather passing through the welter revolutionary Bavaria must have been in late 1918. I tried to remember that I had other plans, and that the incomplete was to my mind an end in itself, a state of lasting tension— like a photograph of a skydiver moments before they leave the open plane door, a long musical note played between the earth and outer atmosphere. I assured myself that the self was indeed an illusion, autonomy a lie we told the emptiness within, trying to remain stable for a short breath of cosmic time, the fluid rhythms we liked to brand 'subjectivity."

I travelled from Coburg to Würzberg, wondering if my grandfather had walked that way in the winter of 1918. But I also had another agenda on my mind: to stand on the Platz in front of the Würzberg Residenz, site and subject of a disputed photograph Sebald includes in *The Emigrants*. It is part of Max Ferber's story, the German exile painter and former *kindertransport* subject whom the Sebald narrator befriends and spends long hours listening to—in a kind of rehearsal of the pattern of *Austerlitz*. Ferber recalls his uncle showing his father a newspaper clipping, supposedly from 1933, with a photograph of a book burning on the Residenzplats. The photograph, reproduced in Sebald's book, shows a corner of the palace in the top left—I could in fact, and did, stand in the exact position the photograph would have been taken from. The bottom half of the photograph was filled with a large crowd, and between the crowd and the Residenz, around the very centre of the photograph, rose a column of white smoke, billowing to the right, presumably from the burning books. Ferber's uncle, however, insists the photograph is a forgery, and indeed there is something not quite right about it. The book burning did take place, there is no disputing that, but there must not have been a serviceable photographic record, so some Nazi propagandist fabricated this document, thereby faking a real event. Ferber's uncle is outraged—but why? Everything about the Nazis was a performance, it was all fake from the start, he says. But there is something else here: that one should be true to the horror that *did* take place? Or, conversely, that there are truths so terrible only fiction can reveal them? I wasnt sure, but Sebald tells us that, in visiting Würzburg, he went to the archives and confirmed Ferber's unclës suspicions. Standing there on the platz, imagining smoke and burnt books, a dizziness overcame me as I stooped to take a photograph of the cobblestones at my feet—right where the books had been burnt. I felt as though I had witnessed the end of the world, but was

none the wiser. The Mayan civilization rose and fell before me, Diego de Landa burning all the Mayan codices, the *auto de fé* taking place before the church in Maní, 1562—although the Mayan alphabet would later be reconstructed, ironically, from de Landās own inquisitorial notes. The Maya believed time to be circular, their own demise having occurred three times already. Climate change, ecological over-reach, exhausted soils, malnutrition (bones become porous and weak), internecine war, and then colonial contact, disease, dispossession— naturally occurring and man-made factors intertwine, form feedback loops. The more energy a civilization can process, the more complex it becomes; lose energy sources or the capacity to process increasing energy demands, and complexity is lost too, the fall begins, the jungle swarms up and over the temples of Tikal and Copan. Or consider the case of Easter Island (Rapa Nui), not laid waste by an out of control cult of ancestors and the supposed mania for carving massive statues in their honour, but, as usual, destroyed by European intervention: the population decimated by disease, press-ganged into the crews of whalers, captured as slaves or set to work, the last few dozen of the islandš native inhabitants, tending imported sheep for mainland ranchers. Here the Indigenous Rapa Nui developed their own system of written glyphs—perhaps one of the few independent inventions of writing in world history— preserved now on a few indecipherable wooden tablets kept in scattered museums, none on the island of their origin. And then there was the effect of the earthš axial procession on the

Sahel (the Arabic word means *coast* or *shore*—the southern border of the great sand sea of the Sahara, transition zone to the rolling savannah), fertile lands desiccated, the ancient library city of Timbuktu on the shores of that endless desert, listening to the Simoom or poison wind, persecuted by the rulers of the Songhai Empire (centred along the Niger river, feeding slaves and gold north to European and Middle Eastern markets, their caravans snaking endlessly across the sands), the ancient texts lost or sometimes hidden in cellars from their attackers, until that civilization too fell into dust.

I moved quickly into the Residenz, if for no other reason than to get out of the sun. The grand baroque building, erected for the Prince-Bishop of Würzburg, was finished in 1744, complete with an elaborate Treppenhaus (stairway hall), just inside the main entrance, on the left, giving access to the apartments above. A massive financial penalty paid by an embezzler to the state of Würzburg provided the funds for the palace—which some claimed rivaled even Versailles—as well as Giovanni Battista Tiepolŏs artists fee for painting the Treppenhaus's remarkable vault. His 600 square meter fresco, covering the entire ceiling above the grand stairs, representing the heavens and the four continents of the world, is Tiepolŏs masterpiece, likely the largest painting in Europe, finished in 1753 when the painter, assisted by his sons, was 57 years old (the same age as Sebald at the time of his death—and mine at the time of this visit). It is so large that it cannot be seen whole from any angle;

it has no frame; it has no narrative centre (and Tiepolo had little taste for narrative in general); to see it one cannot remain still, but must walk—on the stairs and landings or around the gallery, which the stairs access, beneath it. It was said of the Venetian that he worked particularly well in places of passage—waiting-rooms, entrance halls, stairways—things seen according to the rhythms of movement. The taking in of a Tiepolo assumes a mobile eye; it assumes that our moments of transit and transition are often our most significant states of being. The typical function of painting—concentration and legibility—is given over to diffusion and indeterminacy. Lacking the habits of authority and command, Tiepolo frees us to wander and, in so doing, make up our own minds. Which is exactly what I was prepared to do, as I stood at the bottom of the first flight of stairs. Gazing up from this position I saw the large windows of the gallery, and rising from above these, my first glimpse of a portion of the fresco—the frieze representing *America*, and above this, curving onto the ceiling of the vault, a light blue sky with clouds lit in various pinks, until the explosion of gold radiating from the sun god Apollo. I thought of something I had read—that Tiepolo had an excessive love of light, which stole from his shadows. At this point I could see maybe half of the actual ceiling and its heaven; as I slowly climbed the steps (they are low, not much more than four inches rise each step, and broad), keeping my eyes on the vault above, I began to take in more detail. All the human figures in

America are active: carrying, moving, gathering, bearing their various loads—a cornucopia, a bright drum catching the sun, a basket on a woman's head, a dead alligator thrown over a man's shoulder, its white belly shining upwards. There are deer, a bow held up ready to let fly its arrow, standards moving in the wind. *America*, personified as a great queen in feathered headdress, turns her head one way, while pointing in another. There is, perhaps, a volcano in the distance. A tree rises near the centre of the tableau, its branches disappearing into a dark cloud, as though it were a smoldering torch, the cloud lightening as it rises onto the ceiling where luminous gods will sport. Tiepolo, it's said, learned his clouds not by studying nature, but by looking at Veronese; his retreat into minor genres and transitional spaces was characteristic of the latecomer to a tradition. Veronese's style was simply in the Venetian repertoire, and Tiepolo could perform it well. He never travelled to Rome or Florence; their particular traditions were relatively unknown to him. He worked his way back and forth across Northern Italy, like a caged animal, only crossing the Alps north, late in life, over the Brenner pass, for his three years in Franconia, lying beneath this ceiling. For him, Veronese *was* Painting; he borrowed liberally, but I'm sure like myself, he would have refused the term *pastiche*, preferring instead to see it more as a matter of *commoning* shared resources. Or as poet Lisa Robertson has it, to write is to *augment* what others have written: The augmenter is the one who inserts extra folds into the woven substance of language." In taking up his predecessor's manner, Tiepolo shackled himself to a style that paradoxically freed him. I walked on, turning at the halfway point landing to complete the ascent to the gallery in the other direction, where Mercury, in the heavens opposite Apollo, and oriented in the other direction, capered above *Europe*. So the whole of the heavens turned with me as I made my own turn halfway through my ascent. But by now, as I gained the top of the stairs at the gallery, where the windows let light spill in on three sides, like footlights beneath the great fresco, everything could be seen, so long as I kept moving, kept turning. The Treppenhaus is a sort of maze, really, moving through which one catches only glimpses and changing angles of the massive work above. Despite its glowing heavens, the Treppenhaus fresco is in fact entirely earth-bound, and as one ascends the stairs, one *descends* from heaven to earth; the continents and their numerous figures, with their curious detachment, become the focus. The interior lighting of the picture itself interprets the actual lighting outside the building (east and west, the orientation of the windows, matter in this regard); fact and fiction are coeval; inside and outside communicate. The figures, too, respond to onës actual movement through the Treppenhaus, by moving themselves—an effect of the fact that the frieze surface is concave and tilted. Mobility is method. The figures never stand ram-rod straight at attention: they are turning, bending, twisting, rotating, leaning, reaching, lifting, falling, sprawling. *Asia*, a turbaned figure that recalls perhaps a sultan or a mogul, twists to gaze over her should, one arm raised as though to shade her beautiful face from the sun, her body, side-saddle atop an elephant, facing the opposite direction. Around her, from left to right, a palm tree, tiger hunt, slaves, a host bearing gifts, assorted other figures beneath an obelisk, an inscribed block of stone, a man holding a round sun shade aloft, a staff encircled by a snake. Opposite is *Africa*, with many similar motifs: merchants and men loading cargo, camels, an ostrich, a monkey, the radiant black queen herself draped in white, reclining as she gestures to her left, a tent behind her, another parasol held aloft nearby, an allegory of the Nile as an old bearded man leaning back and towards the queen, an oar across his lap and an egret at his side. As has been noted, counter to iconographic tradition, Tiepolo has his camels in Africa and his elephant in Asia, reversing the standard association. This would seem to be in keeping with the informal and asymmetrical arrangement of the various tableau in general: the continents are not sealed from each other; this is a world on its way to being overrun by global traffic; everyone is moving towards mixture and exchange, for better or for worse. I found myself asking, as I circled the gallery again and again, my neck growing stiff, does Tiepolo manage to avoid what we might now see as a superficial gesture of inclusivity—beautiful and noble people from different global backgrounds, in some imagined version of their traditional ethnic costume, singing the same song, unity appropriated for purposes of commodification (despite our differences, we all unite to enjoy Benneton or Coke)? In other words, is his depiction of the four continents simply run-of-the-mill Orientalism? It was hard to deny. But I did have two further thoughts on the matter. For one thing, I could not help feeling that the specific figures were in some way subordinate to a more general function: the making visible of our image-making faculty, our picturing mind at work. There were so many pictorial absurdities: the stovepipe hat on one of the burly merchants in *Asia*, *America* riding in on a huge crocodile, and the absurd colonial figure nearby in European garb, his legs dangling below the pictorial plane while he falls headlong and perhaps greedily into what has been interpreted as a cannibalistic feast in the painting. Much madness makes divinest sense, perhaps. And then there is *Europe* itself, the fourth continent. A horse, a temple, a construction site, musicians playing cello and violins, a striding explorer wrapped in his cloak, canon, and a dog investigating the reclining figure of Balthazar Neumann, the architect of the Residenz. Europa herself reclines on a sumptuously draped throne, largely in shadow; near her, the allegorical representation of art, a woman in a bright crepe and canary gown (much the same shades as the clouds above the scene), leans in, her gaze fixed on the queen, a palette in one hand, and her brush in the other. The brush touches a large globe, painting the world, we can only assume, in *Europe's* image.

Europe is, unlike the three more supposedly exotic continents, overfull, crowded even. Its figures are thus more posed, less active; it is also the only frieze that seems to demand a stationary viewpoint: from below, half-way up the stairs, on the landing at the mid-point, rather than mobile in the gallery. I had another reading too, that it revealed not *Europe* as centre with the other continents as peripheral tributaries, but *Europe* as primordial density collapsing in on itself, a black hole from which the light of another continents, and even the heavens above, would not be able to escape, but into whose void all would be drawn and destroyed. It was many hours before, tired, stiff necked, but filled with a peacefulness I had not felt since my travels began, I finally turned to leave. I paused one last time at the head of the stairs to consider Tiepolōs self-portrait, which I had almost overlooked. Characteristically, it was tucked away, partially hidden in the mouldings and statuary of a corner, right between *Africa* and *Europe*—an appropriate place, I thought, for a Venetian, whose true home was the middle sea. Indeed, he looked, to me, like a sailor: simple red cap, loose yellow scarf, a pole rising behind him, his sons arrayed around as if for voyage, his eyes set on what one could only imagine was the horizon, somewhere outside the room, outside his own masterful painting.

It was then I remembered that the Residenz had been badly damaged by allied bombing during the war; parts of the structure had been burned and ceilings had collapsed. And yet somehow Tiepolōs ceiling fresco was undamaged, the Treppenhaus left intact—even if its stairs now led to nonexistent wings and missing rooms. Even now, decades later, some parts of the building seemed to be under permanent renovation, though whether something was being slowly demolished and removed, or finally completed, I could not tell.

PROPHECY: A DIPTYCH

What might a cloud of mustard gas have looked like from the air, billowing across the earth of No Man's land from one long jagged scar in the earth to another? Great War battle sites were annihilated landscapes, pounded clean of life and feature, *the earth itself corpselike*. In some places the soil has remained toxic for a century—near Verdun, for instance, a sort of forbidden forest was planted and allowed to cover the former battlefield, "as if the men had simply set down their weapons," Cal Flyn writes in *Islands of Abandonment*, "laid down on the earth, and turned into trees." "In that forest there is a clearing—a wound, really—where nothing much will grow. It is called the *Place à Gaz*, the site where, after the war, unused ammunition and chemical weapons were piled up and burnt. It is still a scar, badly scabbed over. At its centre," Flyn writes, "a tar-like ash lies dark and bare," comprised of arsenic, zinc, and lead. Around its edges, only common velvet grass and a lichen, *Cladonia fimbriata*, grow.

Fabrice Monteiro, an Agouda-Belgian and Dakar-based artist, created a series of photographs whose enormous yet elegant subjects rise from the material of their environments like Scamander assuming human form from the waters of the river he also is. Somewhere between fashion photography and photo conceptualism, Monteirõs images of West African figures tower above devastated landscapes: one is covered in black tape, holding a burning torch above mounds of electronic waste; another seems to have formed herself from a smoking landfill, her skirt a composite of the trash rising up around her; yet another, at the meeting point of human and more-than-human forms, appears to be the living emanation of bark and waste-wood, gazing at the last leaf it has lifted from a scorched plane. I wouldnt say Monteirõs images are hopeful; they are more elegiac than anything else; they portend the desperate futures of desperate presents—but they do at least portend futures, however improvised and clipped.

ARGUMENTATION WITH REGARD TO THE FACTS AND RIGHT

I am wondering about facts, evidence, and proof. Which always leads me to poetry, where we speak of *poetic licence*. Which is to say, things show their *true* forms as they slant through poetry. *True* as in: to give the precise form or position. Susan Howe: Poetry has no proof nor plan nor evidence by decree or in any other way. From somewhere in the twilight realm of sound a spirit of belief flares up at the point where meaning stops and the unreality of what seems most real floods over us. 'Belief as in, I believe my grandfather to have suffered. As in, I believe my grandfather to have suffered in the service of one of the most destructive processes in history. As in, I believe all this to be true, both despite and in fact of its complexities and contradictions.

There is a recording, supposedly made at the exact moment the armistice came into effect, 11AM on November 11, 1918. It's maybe not quite two minutes long. The guns are firing, shells whistle and the deep sound of explosions resonate, with machine gun fire chattering at a different pitch. Then the guns go quiet. A few echoes, one late shell that had been waiting to fall, booming deep in the distance. Then silence. And then, after the shortest pause, the sound of a nightingale singing, rising over the fields.... It's a fake. The *recording* is actually an artillery sound ranging, which records the intensity of noise, to determine distance, on photographic film, the result being something like the jagged line a seismograph produces. An artist has, after the fact, added the particular sounds of guns and bombs, following the levels of the sound ranging, performing the score with pre-recorded ballistic instruments. The addition of the nightingale at the end is—poetic license— an imaginary of the sound of peace. Etel Adnan writes that

> our survival depends on
> the capacity of the real to escape
> the assault of language.

I am here, a poet on a long foray into prose, to escape the assault of language—via language. My grandfather flew almost daily from the middle of March 1917 until early August. How did he stay alive? First World War pilots did not live long—usually only a few weeks. His logbook records no kills, and later family lore has him critical of those who boasted of their tally and were lauded as aces. Maybe my grandfather was just lucky. Maybe he was skilled, or cautious. Or a coward. Or maybe he simply figured out how to stay alive: drift above it all, keeping cloud between you and your *enemy*. His logbook entry for 24 June reads simply: *shot down and crashed*. He wound up upside down and with his front teeth knocked out, scores of spent bullet shells rattling around inside the canvas body of the plane, but lucky to have been downed behind allied lines. He is in the air again the next day, his comment in the logbook simply *new machine*. The closing page of his logbook frequently notes *vis poor*, and records enemy planes *attacked, driven off,* or *driven down*. He is often flying at great heights—16,000 feet on the 6th and 8th of August, 19,000 on the 9th. How easily did he breathe up there? Why would he have flown so high? His last entry is 9 August 1917; the next day engine trouble forces him down behind enemy lines; he would spend the next sixteen months as a prisoner of war; as German soldiers approached his downed plane, he climbed out of the cockpit and jumped up and down on its wings, trying to do as

> In the name of the King!
> Sentence
> In the trial against the English prisoners of war
> 1. Capt. Douglas Collis, 2. Lieut. Raymond Schreiber, 3. Lieut.
> Edward Halford, 4. Lieut. Arthur Hicks, 5. Lieut. Michael
> Woods interned at the officers' camp at Bad-Colberg
> accused because of perseverance in disobe-
> dience against a repeatedly given order in ser-
> vice-matters and because of express refusal of
> obedience committed on active service and in
> presence of several soldiers a high court-martial
> composed by the Royal Command of the 11th
> army-corps at Cassel in a session on the

much damage to the craft as he could before he was taken. Amongst my grandfather's papers are several versions, some in German, some in English translation, some typed and some hand written, of his court-marshalling at Bad Colberg. There had apparently been several *attempts of forcible escape*, and as a result, the five prisoners in question were ordered to report in person to the camp Commandant's office at regular intervals throughout the day. It may be that the prisoners were unwell—likely they were underfed—as this was seen by them as a cruel punishment, and my grandfather, as the senior officer amongst those upon whom this order fell, refused to have them comply. I cannot help taking a little pride in his *persistence in disobedience and expressive refusal of obedience*. Family legend, once again, tells of attempts to cut through camp fencing, and the digging of a tunnel, complete with narrow walls shorn up with bed slats and clandestine disposal of excavated earth, that seems like a Hollywood movie, but was in fact not uncommon in various POW camps. However that may be, the men were sentenced to six months *fortress confinement (the Veste Heldberg being the closest and most likely site).* I have no information that confirms that this sentence was carried out, but it seems likely; an appeal was refused in a document issued by the Court of the 11th Army-Corps at Cassel, dated 31 July 1918, when there was still over three months before the war would end and the prisoners were, apparently, simply allowed to wander away.

Further verification of some of these details came in the form of a breezily written memoir by F. W. Harvey, a British soldier and poet held at Bad Colberg at the same time as my grandfather. Like a character out of Blackadder, Harvey seems to have found POW life a lark. There is butterfly hunting, tennis, and "a good prison paper" called the *Morning Walk*. Harvey recounts the attempted escape, the punishment, and with much self-satisfaction, relays how he outwitted the camp Commandant and avoided the court-martial faced by my grandfather and four others. Harvey names no one but confirms that "my friends" were sentenced to "six months' imprisonment in a fortress."Two of those later escaped, and were brought back to the Bad Colberg camp quite dead,"he adds dryly.

I look at my grandfather's Kipling on the table in front of me. Have I declared him guilty by association with poetry? Whatever Kipling means, that meaning is spoken in a lengthy discourse of difference, exclusion and exploitation wherein my grandfather is a small figure simply standing silently in the corner, tending the wheel of a rickety and deadly craft, numbed by technological wonder, preparing to unleash hell, as ordered.

ARCHAIC PLASHING

It would be natural to want to say a word for peace. To channel the Palestinian poet Marwan Makhoul and note that in order to write poetry that isnt political one must hear the birds, but in order to hear the birds, the warplanes would need to be silenced. If I have never known a war zone, I have never known a moment when there wasnt a war zone somewhere—and never known a moment when people somewhere were not yearning for peace. Love and Strife, Eros and Eris, two entwined forces constituting our species' push and pull. Even when we are building our human worlds, we are demolishing natural worlds to which we also belong (no one really needed to say). All technology does is make this outsized. All capitalism does is make another's loss the source of our gain.

Always moving away / coming closer. Maybe the border wont be needed anymore, maybe we will all just be good neighbours, lending a hand, offering ours to be theirs because it is theirs as much as it is ours. Or, maybe the borders will keep growing into the carbon skies, splitting heaven, maybe we will refuse sustenance, deny all connection and relation, let the vast and swelling populations of the nations of not-us fall—some of them into heaven / some of them into hell. My ears stop ringing, and a new sound presents itself. Somewhere in a cool courtyard, a shaded arcade running behind what can be seen, the soft sound of water. It bubbles and flows. It echoes on ancient stones near a lemon tree where a bird alight is just now getting ready to sing.

OPEN THE WINDOW, FROM THESE LAST DAYS ONWARD I CAN FLY

What is an ancestor? A brief pause in the continuous flow of forms and information, a snapshot of something that is in perpetual motion and transformation. I personally have no recollection of my grandfather, but my grandmother I remember from weekly visits to her with my father. She is, in my memory, always in bed, unable to stand or walk, busy trying to be proper and to hold on to the accent from a country she left as an infant. She made tea from her bed, offered biscuits, and looked sadly out through her horn-rimmed glasses. Most mysterious of all to me then was the grey wig that sat on a stand—a vaguely head-shaped bulb—beside her bed, and how I could perceive no difference between the wig and my grandmother's own real hair—not in terms of their colour (white), volume, or overall shape. I also vaguely wondered what had become of the dummy-head's body, and whether it was once attached, and later severed for its present use. There was a small painting on the wall, which she had painted, of an old woman hunched in a doorway, with a pile of potatoes to peel. I hardly knew where to turn. But then, I remembered my grandfather's sister Elsie, a Nursing Sister who crossed with him in 1915, and who kept a diary, the current whereabouts of which I have no idea, although numerous scholars have cited it at length as an authentic first-hand account of a woman's experience of the Great War. First she records parading in her bright blue uniform, with its brass buttons and scarlet collar, through the streets of Victoria and, after crossing from the island on the Princess Sophia, through Vancouver's streets too, bands playing and crowds gathered to send them off. The train took them to Montreal at the end of August, and then the crossing to England where in Plymouth harbour, British sailors cheered as they arrived; by January she would be stationed at Canadian General Hospital No. 5 in Salonika (Thessaloniki) Greece, where the injured from Gallipoli and other eastern theatres were taken. On the way through the Mediterranean, their ship stopped at Malta (after its captain had momentarily mistaken Lampedusa for the larger island), where they bought oranges in the market and visited churches—perhaps for a moment stepping into the shadows of a large Caravaggio, its depiction of blood and sacrifice a warning of what was to come. They stopped next at Alexandria in Egypt, moving inland (I wonder why?) and staying for a time at the elegant Semiramis Hotel on the banks of the Nile in Cairo; the nurses rode camels and visited the great Pyramids, from which escapade they had to make a hasty retreat when some drunk Australians angered the natives. In Salonika the heat was devastating, though the nurses were never seen without their long heavy skirts (Elsie records watching some Greek men swim in the Aegean, their bathing trunks noticeable by their absence). One day the city was bombed by a German zeppelin, which was subsequently shot down in a ball of flames, the burning men jumping to their deaths—a sight Elsie describes with horror and sorrow. A photograph shows another Canadian nurse standing on the wreckage.

By May 1917 Elsie is stationed at Canadian General Hospital No. 1 at Ètaples (which the British called Eat Apples)', France, on the coast of the English Channel, some sixty kilometers west of Arras. On May 19 she lived through a terrible air raid. It was a beautiful night, she writes, stars shot over the dark of the land and the bright sea—as luminous as day. Before dinner I heard distant guns but thought nothing of it. I had just got to the kitchen door when the bombs began to drop. Several fell in the mess quarters and set the row of huts afire. Two dropped outside the nurses club, another outside our new quarters. The whole place was a wreck—poor little Bob was buried with a fractured femur, a huge wound in her other leg and several smaller ones. Miss McDonald was killed. She had a tiny wound but it must have severed the femoral artery as she died of haemorrhage almost immediately. The wounded were taken to G ward, Elsie writes. Several bombs dropped on the officer's lines, on top of Hill 60. Killed one M.O. who was standing up with several others, star gazing I assume. There were about six of us in the kitchen on the floor. It was dreadful. We could see the fires through the window, hear the men shouting and calling. Hear bombs dropping, the guns would all stop for a minute until the machines came within range. All one could hear was their continual buzzing—then the guns again, then the bombs. The windows all fell in, dishes kept breaking, and the plaster walls fell down in places. We were sure the next one would hit us. When there was a lull, we hurried back to the wards. One badly hurt man had been brought to hut X almost dying—three planes returned—one dropped several bombs then left us alone. Several of the hill wards were hit, one destroyed. Where the HSD men slept a number were killed and as many wounded. The OR was busy the rest of the night. Private Wilson was killed. In the coming days Elsie would write about the burials of her comrades and the endless parade of the dead. Bob buried at 3 ŏclock, she writes. We all went to the funeral. It was dreadfully trying. Forty-six boys were buried together in one long grave. Leaving the little field I noticed, I'm not sure why, but I noticed a bright little plant growing beside the path. It was the only one not completely trampled there, the only one passing crowds, and the men carrying the dead to burial, had somehow avoided. It was a small lavender shrub, its spears notably straight and fresh. I smiled, perhaps a little sadly, at the thought of the lavender oil, which we used as a sedative, disinfectant and anti-bacterial in our hospitals, coming from this little plant. The purple flowers jutted up and out, but at the same time kept close to the straight stalk they climbed, as though they were tiny crystals encrusted along its upper spires. I dont know how long I stood there, somewhat stunned and overcome by everything that had happened. But all I could think was how glad I was the little plant was growing there, how its fragrance seemed the very opposite of death when it filled our camp kitchen, a pot of oil boiling on the burner, the bunches of lavender hung nearby, and when a small yellow bee appeared and began landing on one stalk after another, climbing up and down their spires, I thought of the sweetness of the honey that bee would make, and the collaboration going on between plant and animal—a collective effort that long preceded this war, and would last long after it, as a kind of minor monument to the smallest of perseverences.

BEFORE THE SPARK REACHES THE DYNAMITE

In a dream I am at the university and we are all lying on the floor in sleeping bags listening within the half-light of emergencies and back-up generators. At Bì ziers in 1209, during the Albigensian crusade, with the city surrounded by the Popës army, the Abbot of Cî teaux gave the order to ślaughter them all, the Lord will know His own."Some 20,000 residents, so-called heretics and true believers alike, men women and children, were put to the sword in the bloodbath. In 1637 British soldiers from the Connecticut colony surrounded and burnt the Pequot village near Mistick, killing the remaining members of the tribe—some 400 individuals, half of whom were women and children. In October of 2023, Israeli Prime Minister Benjamin Netanyahu betrayed his intentions in Gaza by invoking the biblical reference to the nation of Amalek: Now go and smite Amalek, and utterly destroy all they have, and spare them not; but slay both man and woman, infant and suckling, ox and sheep, camel and ass."Afterwards I come down from the hill, but then realize I have left my mobile phone on campus, perhaps in my sleeping bag. I am in a metro station of sorts, amidst the press of people descending a narrow, ornate, iron spiral staircase, everyone in a hurry pushing forward but someone at the front is injured and descending very slowly—I can see their face grimacing with pain and effort—someone else helping them and I'm trying to calm the crowd down and get them to understand—war harms us all, directly and indirectly, and we can only move as quickly as the slowest amongst us. At the bottom I find myself at the back of some row housing, an overflowing, narrow and slow moving brook close beside me and spreading into its grass verges—where do I go? Around the other way someone says—the water turning and dark, welling through the grasses, silent and full—and I go and I'm on a street in some vaguely European city, broad pavement and the stones of ancient buildings, still looking for the station and my way back up the hill.

TREES COME TO THEIR SENSES

For years I made a regular pilgrimage of visiting the aging poet Phyllis Webb, walking to the ferry and sailing across the Salish Sea to her island home. While Phyllis is gone now, I continue the journey across the narrow sea to visit my mother, born only a few years after Phyllis, and now nearing the age at which the poet chose to depart at last. These visits have become urgent and frequent because, in her mid-nineties, my mother has succumbed to dementia, manifesting as proliferating paranoid delusions. She seems sharper, more present and intense, than ever—it's just that most of what she says is not born up by the facts of our so-called shared reality. She is worried, terrified even: the nursing staff at her care home are involved in organized crime, drugging her and keeping her captive, stealing her things only to return them later, fundamentally altered, or replaced by similar, duplicate items—an embroidery magazine, a favourite sweater—that she knows are not the exact ones she had before. She sleeps in the day so she can stay up at night and surprise the thieves. She plots and conjectures, analyses every detail of reality for the telltale signs of imposters, doubles, the false masquerading as the true. Reading whatever book she has to hand, she annotates the pages carefully, underlining and making notes. She is difficult to distract. Her terrors get the best of her and she assaults one of her care providers, swinging her cane like a club; the police are called and my mother is removed to a hospital to await her fate.

One day, out of the miasma of anti-psychotic meds, she simply says the word poetics. "I dont know if I've ever heard her say the word before, nor do I recall saying it (it's a word I might use) in front of her. She tells me it bothers her that she has an incomplete piece of embroidery that, when she gets better, she says, she will complete. Green threads fade into blank expanse of unstitched linen. I look at her atrophied hands, knowing she hasnt held thread and needle in years, wonder at this late ambition, this desire for completion. The television blares the news—almost every house in Gaza has been knocked to the ground—I turn it down and try to calm her. Her hospital room, at least, has a remarkable view (unobstructed by mesh or grating) onto open countryside, from the sixth floor, so I try to distract her with that. The tops of hemlock trees nod level with our gaze in a gentle breeze, soft and lush with new spring growth. She points at the trees, fumbling for the right words. The're ... the're ...."Hemlocks, I suggest? No," she says, frowning. The're ... perfect."

ZOO STATION

History repeats itself
a tired truism but
repetition's in our DNA
spiralling open and closed
open and closed in a
sort of sewing motion and
I cant help coming back to it
not always as farce after tragedy
too often its tragedy after tragedy
really im just looking for the good
for a salve that doesnt wound
I have only found hints of it
mainly in the living presence
of those history
keeps trying to keep
out of community
the true coalition
as Fred Moten writes
emerges when you
recognize that it's
fucked up for you
in the same way we've
already recognized

that its fucked up for us
I just need you to recognize
that this shit is killing you too
however much more softly
and I'm trying to feel this
as deeply as I can
a pause in the flow
tree leaves moving in the
zoological gardens of Karlsruhe
where my grandfather was a POW
caged on the zoo grounds
human or animal?
it doesnt much matter
we are all animals
but some dont get all the
benefits and dont get to
decide what an animal might
or could be or do—great grace of
this twirling earth embracing us
forest refuge just outside modernism
whatever form of life we take
a pause in the flow
as on a calm moment at sea
a moment of reflection
the sea is trauma for many I know
their most scarring moments
occurred crossing water they

can barely put into words
just say the sea eats them
keeps their memories
below with their bones
and hopes of other worlds
concealed beneath
the wretched of the sea
Achille Mbembe writes
updating Fanon
is this a poem?
I'm not sure but
I'm always curious about
small crafts made of words
made from materials ready to hand
and ready to set sail on thought
or be the thought we sail upon
get us somewhere we need to be
I have a story I want to share
/ just a simple story / hopefully
there will be time to share it
I'm not sure if it's from high
in the air or far out on the sea
that we can best see things whole
see limits and connections
see that the earth has these
various modes of going over
its variegated surfaces

see that all must cross
see that it is the last utopia
(I'm keeping Mbembe close here)
a place of refuge for life
the Earth a true refuge for
humans and non-humans alike
actualized through a multiplicity
of bodies in motion
I doubt my grandfather had time
or mind to think of the shattering
clinging as he was to life
displaced and disintegrating
mechanized and at war with nature
In zoo cages, in fortress confinement
or wandering bereft after disaster
I'm sure he still did not imagine
himself walking in step with
all of wandering brutalized life
I slip from his side—join Osman
wander back   ancestors   the dead
accompany us always
are part of the common life of the Earth
I am Mbembës student
I am Osmans
it's a story of his
I want to get to

/ really just an anecdote /
though the largest pattern
resides in smallest detail
wëll get there still
the truth of movement
the lies we tell of fixity   border   nation
fall away   clinging to an Earth
they would strangle and subdue
Mbembe asks if guilt like trauma
can be intergenerational
Ïm not sure thats whats driving
me here but Ïm curious about
difference and the common
Certainly the rhythm of movement
is not the same for everything or everyone
Mbembe writes *The anti-migration policies*
of the powerful states of the North manifest
this difference clearly, since they contribute

persistently to multiplying the wretched
of the Earth, and increasingly also
the wretched of the Sea
(therës that devouring water again
pulling against drenched clothes)
It is significant (Mbembe continues)
from this point of view, that most contemporary
forms of wretchedness play out at the intersection
of mobility and immobilization

of incarceration and velocity
I know my grandfather's mobility lost
its privileged nature only in war
only temporarily and then returned
to him scarred but able to move in small
circuits constrained back and forth
across coastal waters I'm learning
what we must do is embrace entanglement
the body the Earth and walk in solidarity
with those whose mobilities are proscribed
in the name of difference and scarcity
but how to formulate a we large enough
to include us all—all fucked up being
in its variable fuckedupedness

one (Mbembe again) *that includes*
human beings as well as objects, viruses,
plants, animals, oceans, machines—all the forces
and energies with which we must henceforth
learn to live in bio-symbiosis ...
the greatest obstacle however is racism
the ultimate neurosis of separation. As a singular form
of the war of the species, racism is indeed the exact
opposite of any consciousness of the common
out past the last light houses
a pause in the flow
the little boat in my mind

turning back towards the harbour
if I seek some thin membrane of connection
and solidarity, working from my grandfather's
experience to that of people at the other limit
of colonial legacies, it is not to claim any kind of
knowledge or access or privileged rights
of the suffering—it is, rather, an attempt
to think at planetary scale—to know that
all past separations into lives that matter
and lives that do not are a lie
and that one cannot do anything
without effecting everything else
at some utterly necessary scale
all are connected by the planet we share
but we are running out of time
and tripped up by the contradictions
of our human condition
which Osman illustrated well
for me one day walking together
in the south of England
/ this is the story I wanted to share
just an anecdote really
fragment of his perception /
our path passed along the side of
some well-kept allotment gardens where
at one end we saw a carefully crafted birdhouse
placed high atop a post above beans and tomatoes

and further along we passed one of those plastic owls
(also on a post) meant to scare other birds away
and so protect the delicate flesh of plants beneath
and Osman grabbed hold of my arm, pulling us up short
gesturing excitedly with his eyes wide: see
see—this is exactly what happens:
here they say please come you are welcome
we hope you find this a comfortable home
and here they say do not come or we will kill you
tearing your flesh and rending soft days
and the distance between these points is almost nothing

VERTIGO SEA

Standing in front of Vermeer's *The Geographer*, I wonder what dream of voyages the painting's eponymous figure is staring into as he looks up from his charts, a compass held in one hand, a corner of a map in the other, and looks into the light spilling from the window on his right. His face is expressionless, calculating, seeing the miles to be crossed—and perhaps the profits to be gained. He is young, sumptuously dressed in heavy, thick robes; is it the light of warmer climes he is anticipating? The table beneath his chart is draped with a rug or rich, heavy fabric, piled up in folds, its patterned blues and browns evoking the earth itself, its rumpled surface unsphered and gathered into fungible excess. Teju Cole reminds that no matter how domestically contained Vermeer's scenes appear to be—that one single room whose interior he so often painted—they contain reminders that the world is large, "and that it is a world in which the Netherlands was beginning to make its mark via the maritime dominance of the Dutch East and West India Companies, the latter of which was already (Cole writes) a significant force in the trade in enslaved people."

Frankfurt was a grey portal—a place of entrances and exits. I walked from the Städel Museum, where the Vermeer hung in a room crowded with small Dutch masterpieces, to the Schirn Kunsthalle, crossing the flooding river Main on the Eiserner Steg, a nineteenth century wrought iron footbridge, to the railings of which people had attached thousands of multi-coloured padlocks—as promises of love. Looking towards the Cathedral, I recalled a photograph I had once seen—an aerial view of the heart of Frankfurt taken in 1944, after the city had been fire bombed.

Every building is either a pile of rubble or a fragmented shell formed of broken and roofless walls—only the Cathedral soars above the wasteland, black and inconsolable, but it too is roofless, a dark scorched wreck amidst the shattered town. And yet one could wander through the Römberg today convinced that the Gothic buildings surrounding the market square were indeed centuries old—not replicas rebuilt after the total destruction of the war. This was true of almost every German city I had visited, including Würzberg, the streets and architecture of which had seemed positively medieval, but which had in fact lost 95% of its buildings to Allied bombing. Germany had embraced the replica and facsimile to a disorienting degree. Nothing was exactly what it seemed. The past had to be repeated to a satisfying degree of authenticity, it seemed, but in this replication process, the past was simultaneously preserved and erased: what war had wrought was carefully unmade and time rolled backwards; ruins were not preserved; the fruits of urban labours were rendered unblemished.

I had come to the Schirn—the only reason, in fact, I paused in Frankfurt on my way home—in order to see Ghanaian-British artist John Akomfrah's *Vertigo Sea* (2015), a three-channel colour video installation that, in T. J. Demos' words, shows us the brutal industrialization and militarization of nature."A blue luminescence suffused the dim gallery where the three screens worked their mobile juxtapositions. Seascapes, ice fields, and barren shorelines. Boats slipped over waves, teeming sea creatures filled the depths, and great flocks of gannets dove into cold water or circled plaintively above the sea. Waves filmed from beneath the surface roll past like billowing clouds in the sky. All is pattern and plethora: vast flocks, herds, pods; the natural world filmed richly from above—landscape and light—or as a roiling chiaroscuro from beneath. Murmurations pulsate, a giant flock of birds at one point momentarily assuming the form of a whale in the sky before pulsating onward. But death is beaut⬜s constant companion: polar bears are shot from ship and icefloe, skinned and left flayed on the snow, and whales, which first appear in all their grace and mystery, rolling through light and song, increasingly figure as the bloody victims of whale hunters, complete with voiceover quotations from *Moby Dick* and historical footage of harpoons shot from the bows of boats heaving in rough seas, and sloppy abattoirs of viscera and gut. Perhaps most troubling is the frequent juxtaposition of these scenes of hunting and slaughter with evocations of the Atlantic slave trade, including voiceover and images related to the purposeful drowning of enslaved Africans thrown overboard in the Middle Passage—an evocation of or direct reference to the *Zong* incident (although that is just one tragic if emblematic example of the bone-filled hold that the sea had become). An epigraph on screen as a section break in the film quotes Primo Levi: The way of killing men and beasts is the same." We eliminate life, human and non, with the same impunity. The expendabilit⬜ of enslaved Africans is echoed in the film by the fate of contemporary refugees, who are also cast out on the sea, whose voices we hear, and whose bodies wash up on distant shores. There is no narrative centre to the film, and you cannot really take in all three screens at once—mobility and a roving eye is the only method. As the three screens variously show, for instance, frozen landscapes, dense misty forests, and golden flocks of monarch butterflies, a lone boat might appear amidst waves, a whale's vast but limp body will be shown being sliced open from stem to stern, or a historical photograph of an enslaved man or child's face in extreme closeup suddenly fills one screen, looking the viewer directly in the eye.

While much of the footage is derived from various documentary sources, a series of recurring Rückenfigurs are clearly staged scenes with actors. One of these figures is a black man wearing the three-cornered hat and redcoat of a British officer—a figure identified with Olaudah Equiano, born in what is now southern Nigeria, former slave, memoirist, and anti-slavery activist (1745-1797). The other such figures, usually alone or as a distracted and distanced pair, appear to represent settlers of some kind: they are Europeans, by dress from various epochs of the colonial age, dressed in their contemporary formal high fashions but isolated on barren headlands and desolate shores. They are dressed more for society than the wilds they are portrayed in, and are often accompanied by their bourgeois objects—desks, lamps, chairs, a bed frame, books and framed paintings, or, in evocations of later periods, a typewriter, and a bicycle and a baby's pram (up to their wheels in the surf of a beach)—scattered amongst coastal rocks, grasses, and headlands. Sometimes they are in tears; often they are accompanied by or holding clocks (whose ticking *Vertigo Sea* begins with). The time of colonization is the time of the Anthropocene—the era of the human demolition of the planetary ecosystem, the time of "modern logistics," as Fred Moten and Stefano Harney write, founded on the first great movement of commodities, the ones that could speak.'I think Equiano, who always appears alone and usually at a distance, amidst thundering natural landscapes, is the focalizer of all of this: like Tiresias *in The Waste Land*, he sees all, is witness to the vastness of the catastrophe human beings have wrought— the deaths of enslaved Africans, polar bears, whales, and the more casual cruelties of the oblivious colonizer. But the settler figures are interesting too; are they shipwrecked, with their belongings hauled ashore and hastily piled up (an upside down chair on a desk, beside open books and charts to be poured over as in Vermeer's *Geographer*). They are sad, inconsolable even, forlorn and out of place. They are unsettled, in a state of stasis amidst a film of mobilities, uncertain of where they belong. Noteworthy is the repeated presence of a golliwog, a cloth doll of exaggerated racialized features, either in historical footage of playing (white) children, or as one object amongst the settler's shored clutter. What is the message here? A reminder that the increasing global mobility of peoples is always racialized and accompanied by racisms of various degrees of horror and intent? Every image in *Vertigo Sea* relates to sea crossing, whether by boat-born human beings or migratory birds or whales, and every human figure—soldier, enslaved African, migrant, fisherman or colonist—is someone who has set out, by choice or not, on thunderous seas. Demos describes Akomfrah's "cinema of relationality," which "reveals unanticipated connections between narratives, none of them complete." The sea brings everything into relation, rendered by Akomfrah via "montages fundamentally migrant image" (Demos again); the artist himself concurs, noting that "on one level, all I'm doing is just alluding to the coexistence of these things." There is perhaps a scale of mobilities on which all life might be arrayed, allowing the viewer to see both the connections between diverse movements (bird migration and the transatlantic slave trade), and the coalescence of deadly patterns—the butterfly effects of single whaling voyages or a single family's migration, and racial genocide, global warming, and total war, for instance. Place your own family history on this spectrum. Live in the truth that, however tiny you may feel, for better or for worse each of us has a part in the dramatic sweep of earthly rearrangements. Even if all we did was receive a racist toy from our confused parents— or a book of colonial propaganda disguised as poetry.

And so my paternal grandfather, who took his part in what Walter Benjamin called (in oblique reference to the Great War) "this immense wooing of the cosmos," which "was enacted for the first time on a planetary scale—that is, in the spirit of technology," as "aerial space and ocean depth thundered with propellers, and everywhere sacrificial shafts were dug in Mother Earth."The Great War was great not for any high imperial drama or sense of noble cause but because it had become for the first time an Earthly War, a Great and General War on the Planet itself—*upon* and *against* the totality of what physics and evolution had produced. From this grand horror my grandfather escaped onto the sea, in pursuit of what Osip Mandalstam referred to as the dream of being free of tedious intermediaries, so that human being and cosmos might at last be left alone with each other. He leapt into a boat where some leapt into volcanos. Perhaps it was his plane that was supposed to have ferried him across to a landing field beyond, filled with asphodels; statistics suggest it should have; the boat he set out on almost daily for the rest of his life was a form of perpetual wandering, voyaging the seas forever more, without respite, a curse for having failed to make the correct landing on the shore beyond, a compulsion of otherworldly origin as he took on the roles of silent ancient mariner and aging, solitary Ulysses, striving yet not seeking, the form of his eternal exile chosen for him—not to be a pilot, but forever merely the ferryman. A voice inside me was speaking. Do we lack faith in the consistency of daily life? We do. Or we should, if we look closely enough. A stable life might depend on not looking too closely; we may find ourselves not singular, but multiple—a tangle of others—projections, fantasies, delusions, quotations, unconscious appropriations—we cobble a self together and pawn it on the open market of social interactions. Those lines in your head—did you read them, or write them? Are they—*your'n*? That history—whose record, and whose ritual? What if what life gives us is discrete and decontextualized facts entangled in meshes of collaborative invention? Or—and perhaps it amounts to the same thing— we set out in rafts of selected facts we lash together, crossing seas of collective fantasy? And how is one piece of reality related to another? Simply through the act of our laying them one beside the next, having scavenged them as improvised material for venturing out on invented seas? And what of the real in the end, which seems to wobble every moment more dramatically on the edge of the abyss? Fact and fiction are as quantum waves and particles, a flickering between"(Ben Lerner), both amorphous moments of the structureless jell (Erwin Schrödinger) of the Real. Accompanied by the thunder of propellers, alone in his cosmic wooing, the night sea ready to be lit by whatever light might bring, Percy Douglas remained in perpetual sea-born motion, day in and day out—until he did not wake up one day, long into his 70s, always ferrying some pilot back and forth across unpredictable waters to the ships coming and going with their burden of global *logisticality*. And so I think sometimes I will keep on writing until I too do not wake one day. And what I write is one unfolding and incomplete structure of words, each moment falling into ruin and rising up towards some unimaginable form. What did he imagine about that surface he rode—the liminal sheen between realms above and below? Was it another world down there, the surface of the water its sky? A city of perfect justice on the silty bottom, the sounds of its bells almost audible to those drifting quietly on the other side of their firmament?

PILOT BOAT

Bury me at sea
where no murder ghost can haunt me
—The Pogues

In cold rubble time
in exits and doorways
looking up at
overhead lighting
we called *stars*
though *skygrief*
though *citylight*
or lightless because
sky fire and
house fell down
and yet music
the saturated colours
of certain photographs
how through cold
and rain and the
horror show of wars
we kindle still
we light and hold
welcome the sea

into the sky
sky into sea
to get at that
which is entangled
in each—I mean you
wide-shining daughter
of earth and sky
here we are looking
for a place to land
in the storm
when the pilot
already has swum
back to shore
a blurred cipher
out of mauve morning
through sea crossings
through Akomfrah
flock after flock of
cormorants flecking the
morning sea calm and
quaternary sounds
beginning all those
flagging endings
breeze broken and
calm those thoughts
on this calm water
this swift morning suite

seeing in patterned colour
and light and its variants
cloud-shape the eye
toward foreshores
and atemporal tableau
in perpetual flux
like sound our being
needs motion in order
to exist and I, like you
am a pause in perpetua
the pilot-self we assume
must be there when
really we are all just
ferrymen going back
and forth bearing
who knows what
in the hold our
cinema is molecular
topography teases us
into lingual foment
the essence is movement
wave from your boat
to those on the shore
of a larger vessel called
land or even *Earth*
that waves back
moving in the other

direction its tectonics
molten sea
memory is viscous
and on fire
it burns in sea depths
clogged with corpses
many sail to escape
or carry it with them
like quicksilver it slips
away to denser depths
gone with land and
language that sails away
with the rotating earth
turbulence and dislocation
the intangible memorial
of the sea your friends
vanished into or across
and how much better
across than into though
still pain piles one wave
on top of another and
ghost ships haunt as
coast guard smugglers
and navies repel for
refoulement no right
to light night travels
boats move on beneath

waves and eternity
this memory deep as
empires and just as
chattel-minded
it cant behold in holds
its gaze seeks limitless
water and vista
wants just a now to
becalm in temporal winds
that never let or lull
moments of difference
as desire or desertion
vast as compulsion's seas
the west is always receding
people keep returning
to shore ruins
paltry edifices in times
of utter mobility
carrying clocks to
encountered continents
planet's movement towards
the east ever arriving
the prograde rotation
our feet kick off
we mix and fold
hold each other on
cold shingle stone and sand

land to light or fight on
abandoned towns or the
sound of forced abandonments
gannet after gannet
a feathered bomb shot
into unstilled depths
all hands on deck
the earth is sinking
and where will all this
grasping get us in the round
utopian hopes as harbours
silted up centuries ago
still some firës light
from which others spill
in flight over deserts
just as dangerous as
seas having chased
themselves right the way
round once again the
coasts guard ghosts of
arrival and return fare
the ferryman nods as the
pilot steps off his deck
I'm for the blur and
the bleed-through says
Akomfrah amidst torqued
turbulent time *not in*

harmony but at least
in dialogue with the
skipper of the boat and
the larger entity the sea
swinging and hacking
at the waves
always stretching out and
stretching down in both space
and time along the littoral
we elemental meet to
resist the urge to bisect
even the land and sea
are intimately bound up
one with the other so
they are sometimes in
dense fogs indistinguishable
the sea will wash us
in a secret liquor
a cold fire envelope
and I just wanted to get
myself out of the way
jagged ribs of rocks
out of the dark night
the lights of Lampedusa
lights of ships in flight
the pilot already
swam back to shore

abandonment as beginning
of journeys unending
murmurations pulsating
and perpetually metamorphic
above the port and the
warehouses of the world
the scale of what we
are now responsible for
counters any response
locking up those who
merely sought safety
across dangerous water
tasting salt burns
from leaking fuel
a hum and a whirring
all those lives wildly adrift
a feeling of vertigo
as if I had crossed a wide
stretch of water to a coast
of trees like a heaving sea
the fires never go out
the sense of being
wholly surrounded by water
a vertiginous feeling
the crags rise above the
barque that was to have
ferried him ashore

so that free from
land-based pressures
larger brains evolved
though liquidity and
the grace of unlight
men killed them anyway
where others just wanted
what was elsewhere
and otherwise
imagined new lands
and better lives
not idle roaming (this
is Glissant) *but a sense
of sacred motivation*
or in Mbembës words
*the earth—a vibratorium
forge and granary
womb and cave
home and refuge*
and so you arrive at a sea
called the contemporary
where the eternal present
is a plunge through
stilled waters anointed
with infinite information
and algorithmic
recommendations

but no places and no
times to rend our bodies
into the lived forms
of love and strife
the control of nature
(writes Walter Benjamin)
the sole purpose
of all technology
or so empire teaches
or is it the relation
between what i've been
taught is *inside* me
and what is supposed
to be *outside*
tinkering in troughs
between shoreless swells
as buildings slowly
move about and a
garden suddenly bends
forward and sets off
gracefully into the distance
animal upon animal
the teeming seas of life
as above so below
the tropic of waves
we go into the unknown

having heard our names
called from far out
a full gale unwinding
into the salt dark
its fires nursed and
running white from the bow
gulls in wailing slant
illusioned out of the flood
the sea leaking into the sky
and a beam of sun descending
upon ice, that state between
water and land—is water
we can walk on
memor's arctic coin
and cold membrane
the ice in isolatoes
cooling to our
earthly community
what is the sea and its
creaturely multitudes to us?
bones on the sea bed
feeding the ghost
on new exoskeletal life
above thermal vents
out of burnt earth
the frantic shoal
tore a white gash

in the sea
the frenzy
the blue
the bomb
dropped into water
we thought there were
too many for us to
kill them all
no end to
free abundance
silent acidic seas
iceless arctics
whorls and multitudes
bird density and shack solitude
Jesus save me Jesus save me
echoing from Akomfrah's screen
as invisible one after
invisible other seeks
refuge not return
kiss me with rain
in the end one only
experiences oneself
and the way of killing men
and beats is the same
frame after frame
shoreless, indefinite as god
the land seemed to

scorch his feet so he
set his boat out
the harbour mouth
into the unknown of
machines and thrumming
swinging and hacking
until his dying day
his hands on the wheel
the motor his motive
wide gulfs of silence spread
across yawning sounds
I do not know what I am
for in water's environs
or where I truly belong
surrounded by objects
I've pulled ashore
say I am from empire
descendant of its minor
operatives and I write
to be alone with the abyss
within poetry—poetry
the sea while prose
is a boat though
I cling to its wreckage
its clocks and furnishings
washing ashore
each item incomplete

and turned in on itself
better be a receiver
a listener or small acoustic
space where other voices
resound maybe it's ok
to not be a pilot
and be a ferryman instead
maybe it's ok not to
know the ways the world is
interconnected and know
instead the local waters and
the simple routes out and
back into a single harbour
but know intimately
the never-still
surface of the protean
water there in each ebb and
trough between Trial Island
and Race Rocks

Sources

Adnan, Etel. *Time*. trans. Sarah Riggs (New York, 2019).

Akomfrah, John. *Vertigo Sea* (2015).

Barker, Ralph. *The Royal Flying Corps in World War I* (London, 1995).

Benjamin, Walter. *One-Way Street*. trans. Edmund Jephcott (Cambridge MA, 2016).

Borges, Jorge Luis. "Tlön, Uqbar, Orbis Tertius," *Labyrinths* (New York, 1964).

Bragg, Rick. "The Racist Song That Has Dig Deep Roots in American Culture," *The New York Times* (May 3 2022).

Braudel, Ferdinand. *The Mediterranean and the Mediterranean World in the Age of Phillip II*. trans. Siân Reynolds (New York, 1972).

Calasso, Roberto. *The Ruin of Kasch*. trans. William Weaver and Stephen Sartarelli (Cambridge MA, 1994).

Christensen, Inger. *The Condition of Secrecy*. trans. Suzannan Nied (New York, 2018).

Cooksley, Peter G. *The Royal Flying Corps 1914-1918* (Stroud, 2004).

Crompton, Tom. "Poetics of the Deindustrial Landscape" (University of Warwick, 2024).

David, Tracy C. *The Broadview Anthology of Nineteenth-Century British Performance* (Peterborogh, 2011).

Demos, T. J. "Feeding the Ghost: John Akomfrah's *Vertigo Sea*," *John Akomfrah: Signs of Empire* (New York, 2018).

Duffus, Maureen. *Battlefield Nurses in WWI* (Victoria, 2009).
Dyer, Geoff. *The Missing of the Somme* (Edinburgh, 1994).
Erpenbeck, Jenny. "Homesick for Sadness," *Not a Novel: A Memoir in Pieces*. trans Kurt Beals (New York, 2020).
Flyn, Cal. *Islands of Abandonment: Nature Rebounding in the Post-Human Landscape* (London, 2021).
Glissant, Éduard. *Poetics of Relation*. trans. Betsy Wing (Ann Arbor 1997).
Graves, Robert. *Goodbye to All That* (Manchester, 2007).
Hailu, Gebreyesus. *The Conscript*. trans. Ghirmai Negash (Athens OH, 2013 [1927]).
Hamilton-Paterson, James. *Marked for Death: The First War in the Air* (London, 2016).
Harvey, F. W. *Comrades in Captivity: a Record of Life in Seven German Prison Camps* (London, 1920).
Hassall, Christopher. *Rupert Brooke: A Biography* (London, 1964).
Heraclitus. G. S. Kirk and J. E. Raven, *The Presocratic Philosophers* (Cambridge, 1957).
Herzog, Werner. "Was the Twentieth Century a Mistake," in conversation with Paul Holdengräber (*Brick*, 2009).
Hölderlin, Friedrich. *Essays and Letters*. ed and trans. Jeremy Adler and Charlie Louth (London, 2009).
Hollis, Matthew. *Now All Road Lead to France: a Life of Edward Thomas* (New York, 2012).
Howard, Liz. *Letters in a Bruised Cosmos* (Toronto, 2021).
Howe, Susan. *Frame Structures: Early Poems, 1974-1979* (New York, 1996).
Howe, Susan. *Spontaneous Particulars: the Telepathy of Archives*

(New York, 2014).

Kipling, Rudyard. *Departmental Ditties, Barrack-Room Ballads, and other Verses* (New York, 1899).

Kipling, Rudyard. "Mary Postgate" (1915).

Kipling, Rudyard. "With the Night Mail" (1905).

Lerner, Ben. *10:04* (Toronto, 2014).

Light, Allison. *Common People: the History of an English Family* (London, 2014).

Løgstrup, Johanne. *Co-existence of Times—A conversation with John Akomfrah* (Berlin, 2020).

Makhoul, Marwan. "In order for me to write poetry that isn't political."

Matviyenko, Svitlana. "Vertical Occupation" (*Eurozine*, April 2024).

Mbembe, Achille. *the earthly community: reflections on the last utopia* (Rotterdam, 2022).

Moten, Fred and Stefano Harney. *The Undercommons: Fugitive Planning and Black Study* (Chico CA, 2013).

Nguyen, Vinh. *Lived Refuge: Gratitude, Resentment, Resilience* (Berkeley, 2023).

Nietzsche, Friedrich. *Thus Spoke Zarathustra*. trans. Walter Kaufmann (London, 1978).

Pitts, Johnny. *Afropean: Notes from Black Europe* (London, 2019).

Platonov, Andrey. *Chevengur*. trans. Robert Chandler and Elizabeth Chandler (New York 2023).

Platt, Ellen Spector. *Lavender: How to Grow and Use the Fragrant Herb* (Mechanicsburg PA, 1999).

Rankine, Claudia. "The Condition of Black Life is One of Mourning," *The New York Times* (June 22 2015).

Rimbaud, Arthur. *Rimbaud: Complete Works, Selected Letters.*
 trans. Wallace Fowley (Chicago, 2005).
Robinson, Dylan. *Hungry Listening: Resonant Theory for
 Indigenous Sound Studies* (Saint Paul, 2020).
Robinsong, Erin. *Wet Dream* (Toronto, 2022).
Said, Edward. *Orientalism* (New York, 1978).
Salih, Osman. "The Leader's Tale," *Refugee Tales* Vol. 5
 (Manchester, 2024).
Sebald, W. G. *The Emigrants*. trans. Michael Hulse (New York,
 1996).
Sebald, W. G. "Ghost Hunter," interview with Eleanor Wachtel.
 the emergence of memory: conversations with W. G. Sebald,
 ed. Lynne Sharon Schwartz (New York, 2007).
Sebald, W. G. *Vertigo* (New York, 1999).
Sharpe, Christina. *In the Wake: On Blackness and Being* (Durham
 NC, 2016).
Stepanova, Maria. *In Memory of Memory*. trans. Sasha Dugdale
 (Toronto, 2021).
Thomas, Edward. *Collected Poems* (London, 2004).
Thomas, Edward. *In Pursuit of Spring* (London, 1914).
Thomas, Edward. *The Icknield Way* (Redditch, 2011 [1913]).
Walcott, Rinaldo. "Towards Another Shape of this World,"
 Borders, Human Itineraries, and All Our Relations
(Toronto, 2023).
Wohl, Robert. *A Passion for Wings: Aviation and the Western
 Imagination, 1908-1918* (New Haven, 1994).

Acknowledgements

Many of the titles used throughout *Knock Down House* are taken from Walter Benjamin's *One Way Street*. Some material used in "Pilot Boat" comes from on-screen text in John Akomfrah's *Vertigo Sea*.

The image on p. 25 is my own photograph of Sebald's, the original of which can be found in *Shadows of Reality: A Catalogue of W. G. Sebald's Photographic Materials*. ed. Clive Scott and Nick Warr (Norwich, 2023). The image on p. 134 is "Nursing Sister Emily Edwardess," by J. S. Matthews (1916), City of Vancouver Archives.

Work from *Knock Down House* has appeared in *Free Verse*, *Ludd Gang*, and the Gatwick Detainees Welfare Group Newsletter; thanks to the editors. An early version of some of this material appeared in an essay: "Common Animal Being: A Natural History of Destruction." *Paideuma* 47 (2022): 139-148.

Thanks to David Herd, Cecily Nicholson and Catriona Strang for direction, and Kess Mohammadi for the nudge. Thanks to Osman Salih for his story, shared and reshared between us for many years now. Thanks also to Alvin Collis, Cathy Collis, Robert Leece, Isabella Wang, and Matt Whittle. Thanks to Philip Piper at UAF Upavon.

Thanks to Ghazal Mosadeq for the wonder that is Pamenar Press.